The Other Voice

The Other Voice

Twentieth-Century Women's Poetry in Translation

Edited by

Joanna Bankier · Carol Cosman

Doris Earnshaw · Joan Keefe

Deirdre Lashgari · Kathleen Weaver

Foreword by Adrienne Rich

W · W · Norton & Company · Inc ·

NEW YORK

Copyright © 1976 by W. W. Norton & Company, Inc. All rights reserved.
Published simultaneously in Canada by George J. McLeod Limited,
Toronto. Printed in the United States of America.

First Edition

Library of Congress Cataloging in Publication Data
Main entry under title:

The Other voice.

  Bibliography: p.
  Includes index.
1. Poetry—Women authors. 2. Poetry, Modern—
20th century—Translations into English. 3. English
poetry—Translations from foreign languages.
I. Bankier, Joanna.
PN6109.9.09   808.81'9'352   76–45349

ISBN 0 393 4416 5 cloth edition
ISBN 0 393 04421 1 paper edition

Since this page cannot legibly accommodate all the copyright notices, the
four pages following constitute an extension of the copyright notice.

This book was designed by Jacques Chazaud.
Typefaces used are Palatino and Primer.
Manufacturing was done by Vail-Ballou Press, Inc.

1 2 3 4 5 6 7 8 9 0

To Marsha Hudson

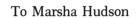

Contents

Being a Woman

Women and Men

Meditations

Speaking for Others

Visions

Foreword

The idea of a common female culture—splintered and di-asporized among the male cultures under and within which women have survived—has been a haunting though tentative theme of feminist thought over the past few years. Divided from each other through our dependencies on men—domestically, tribally, and in the world of patronage and institutions—our first need has been to recognize and reject these divisions, the second to begin exploring all that we share in common as women on this planet. As artists and intellectuals we have often accepted the terms of the male-generated tradition, sensing no alternative. Today, the alternatives are beginning to be unearthed and brought to light. And it is an unearthing. As women, like a tribe long ago conquered and dispersed, we have our buried cities, our pictographs on the walls of hidden canyons, our anonymous songs, our lost arts and tools, our secret sharings, our inscriptions which are only beginning to be deciphered.

The metaphor is archaeological, but in fact the unearthing begins as much today or yesterday as somewhere in history. The poets in this anthology are twentieth, not twelfth-century; yet they have been buried more often than not by the male interna-tional literary establishment which selects the poets to be pub-lished, translated and exported, awards the prizes, edits the an-thologies, writes the literary criticism, and which prefers its women geniuses dead. I have known for years of Ekelöf and Tran-strömer, but not till now of Rydstedt-Dannstedt or Backberger; of Neruda and Paz, but not of Fuertes or Corpi; of Seferis but not of Anghelaki-Rooke or Farrokhzād. Many of the women included here have influenced the poetic traditions and language of their own lands, while remaining unknown to each other. In an age of renewed interest in translation, the women poets of the world have still lacked a real sense of each other's powers. Not just women who write poetry, but the state of poetry itself, and all who look to poetry for greater self-knowledge, have suffered from this ignorance.

This book can only be a beginning: a selection, by one group of western women, of twentieth-century women's poetry in languages other than English, available to them at this time. It offers only a hint of the world-wide efflorescence of poetry by women in this century. Yet even so, its strength and richness are astonishing. It reinforces my sense that women of whatever class, nation or race share a common sensibility—a sensibility that is complex, subversive, and heterodox.

I have been thinking, as I read these poems, how visionary, yet how anti-romantic, we have had to be. Amrita Pritam's testimony on marriage (certainly "My Breadwinner" is a poem of sexual politics); the sense of history, politics and female existence converging in the poems of Forūgh Farrokhzād; Marina Tsvetayeva's unsparing dissection of heterosexual romance in "Poem of the End"; Sarah Kirsch's satire on the domestic life of male poets in "Brief Landing"; Lucha Corpi's great mythic "Marina Poems"— these make a lot of the international poetry in other anthologies, predominantly by men, seem emotionally callow, politically oversimplified. Like any other oppressed group, women have been watching and listening in silence for centuries; we have learned to observe what really happens. As Gloria Fuertes says,

> . . . though tiny, I know many things,
> and my body is an endless eye
> through which, unfortunately, I see everything.

For none of these poets could it be simple to be a poet in a woman's body, that object perceived alternately as sacred and filthy, necessary and loathsome, that chattel of civilization, that machine for reproduction. For a woman to detach herself from prescribed relationships long enough to close a door behind her and sit down to write is still a pressing challenge. The mere sense of identity required has had to be fought for in patriarchal culture, and has been won, if at all, at great cost. It is an enormous statement that Anna Rydstedt-Dannstedt, born in 1928, was able to make:

> I too am born and
> grown to be this thing only:
> to be Anna in the world.

My body is an endless eye. To be Anna in the world. Every
woman included here might say, in Alfonsina Storni's words:

> Maybe all that my verses have expressed
> is simply that which was never allowed to be:
> nothing more than what was hidden and suppressed
> from woman to woman, from family to family.

Every woman included here, Western or Third World, poor or
middle-class in origin, is a "special" woman, one of those who
somehow found her voice and moved out of the silence or the un-
written verbal tradition of women, into the glare and vulnerability
of print. All women, not just those in pre-literate societies, have
shared an anonymous oral tradition. The translations of anony-
mous oral poetry included here suggest that in both hemispheres
women live under certain common universal stresses as women.
But until the last few years, with the emergence of a new world-
wide feminist consciousness and the beginnings of journals and
presses created by and for women (especially in the U.S.), a
woman who has published at all has done so at the mercy of male
approval—and even if published, was read in the light of a male
tradition, her value determined by men. How this fact has af-
fected the themes available to women we are only now beginning
to know as materials and experiences become legitimized that
were formerly discounted as "women's subjects"—therefore triv-
ial or scandalous.
   There are intimations here of a poetry that has always existed
underground and that is now on the verge of a great flowering:
the poetry of women written to and for each other, whether as
comrades, sisters, lovers, or daughters and mothers. There are no
love poems here overtly written from woman to woman; such po-
etry has often been suppressed or forced into code, but we know
it exists and will exist in greater power and quantity as women
become freer to acknowledge intense feelings for each other. But
the driving need of women to speak to each other is clear in these
pages, in poems of great force: Farrokhzād's "Mechanical Doll,"
Karin Boye's "A Sword," Ditlevsen's "Divorce," Backberger's "I'm
Taking Off," Molodowsky's "Women Songs ɪ."
   Why should women poets speak especially to women? Let it be
said here again, as it has so often had to be repeated, that the lit-
erature hitherto described as "human" has been almost exclu-

sively a male monologue—"that long monologue," as the "Three Marias" of the *New Portuguese Letters* style it, "which they have called dialogue with us." The real art or literature of any group comes into being when the members of that group cease feeling the need to explain and justify themselves to a dominant culture and begin to reclaim and create their own culture, for themselves. Women are the one caste which cuts across and forms a majority of every national, political, social, cultural fragmentation into which the species is divided. Patriarchy, with its arbitrary and violent divisions, has denied us our community as women, denied us even our channels of communication where it could. As we now begin to hear and to address each other, the possibility of a real world culture begins.

Therefore in the end a book like this is by no means for women only. The man who sees in poetry by women a means of enlarging his own vision and sensibility, of exploding androcentric ideas of what it means to be "human," will find in anthologies like this one a long-needed resource. What men will do with the new presence of women's images, themes, voices in the world remains to be seen. I am grateful that my sons will be living more and more in the presence of women who are image-makers, namers, sayers of our own words.

One last word on translation: How do we read a collection of translations from so many different languages by so many different hands? The music, the associative patterns within a language, the way certain words, sounds, meanings conflict and resonate within a poem are, if not lost, anyway transformed, transposed, rescored for a different instrument, in the act of translation. In my experience, what carries over most powerfully in translation is the poetic image, the concrete and visionary apprehension of things in the world as the poet absorbs them into her inner life. In a translation which sets out to replicate meter and rhyme at all cost, we are in danger of losing the exact nature of the image, or of seeing it wrenched out of shape to conform to a certain sound-system. The translators for this anthology seem to have felt the same way and to have sought a natural and translucent English unencumbered by laborious imitations of, say, Russian rhyme-patterns. What we receive are the images, in which we touch our profound common experience and recognize certain themes that have obsessed and disturbed us, the dreams of women sleeping everywhere in the world, the visions of women half-awake and waking.

Adrienne Rich

Preface

In 1970 a group of women, many associated with the Department of Comparative Literature at the University of California, Berkeley, came together to study the work of women writers who had been treated summarily or overlooked in the regular academic curriculum. We soon began to discover excellent women poets from ancient times to the present whose work had not been translated into English. To make this poetry available to the group, original translations were undertaken. In 1971 we began to meet on Sunday nights for poetry readings and translation workshops. These meetings attracted a large number of people with unusual talents and language skills who contributed poems in translation from a wide variety of languages, ranging from Byzantine Greek and Classical Chinese to Gaelic and modern Danish. This open group became a forum for people interested in both poetry by women and in verse translation. Translations presented at these reading-workshops became the core of this anthology, which continued to grow and change over the next three years. We limited its scope to the twentieth century, at the same time broadening the cultural and geographical range with the addition of many new poems, some already published, but most of them not. We hope *The Other Voice* will convey some of the enthusiasm and excitement we all felt during the initial Sunday night readings as we worked to shape the book.

We wish it were possible to mention here every person who participated in the various stages of the work; each person's contribution was unique and indispensable, and we would like to thank each one individually. For lack of space we are forced to limit ourselves to a more general and restricted acknowledgement. First, we would like to thank everyone who contributed translations and all the men and women who participated in the group readings. We are also grateful to the many people who introduced women poets unknown to us and provided information about the poets' lives and work. We are especially grateful for the editorial assistance of Kamal Boulatta, Janine Canan, Bridget Connelly, Allan Francovich, Laura Hager-Stortoni, Hope Krauskop, Catherine Rodriguez-Nieto, and Laura Schiff. Thanks also to Georgia Hanouna and Mary Gordon. We would also like to acknowledge the support of the members of the faculty of the Department of Comparative Literature, University of California, Berkeley. Finally, we would like to thank our editor at Norton, John Francis, with whom we worked closely in the final stages of preparation of the manuscript.

A Note on Translation

The poets included in this book come from China and the Far East, Europe, Russia, the Middle East, India, Africa and the non–English-speaking Americas. They write in thirty-one languages which reflect complex geographical, historical and linguistic situations. For example, the Lebanese poets Nadia Tuéni and Venus Khoury write in French, and Etel Adnan in French and English, whereas in most Arab countries the dominant literary language is a modernized form of Classical Arabic. Two of the African poets write in the Portuguese inherited from colonial domination; Ingrid Jonker writes in Afrikaans, the language of the Dutch settlers in South Africa; and Caroline N. M. Khaketla writes in Southern Sotho, the chief language of Lesotho but one which, like many African languages, has only recently become a medium for written literature. The Israeli poets are writing in Hebrew, which was revived as a spoken secular language only at the end of the nineteenth century. In the United States the linguistic situation is also complex. For one thing, immigrant groups have often preserved the language of their native culture. Many Jews from Eastern Europe have continued to write in Yiddish, a German dialect with elements borrowed from Hebrew; and Spanish is of course an active medium for poetry among Puerto Ricans and Mexican-Americans. On the other hand, many American Indian tribes have maintained linguistically distinct traditions of oral poetry. Several of these groups are represented in this anthology.

A book of poems translated from such a variety of languages may seem deceptively simple and accessible to the reader of English. It is important to be aware that these poems in English *are* translations, that they embody a very special kind of literary process. A poetic translation can never reproduce the original poem. If it is faithful to some of the qualities of its model it is likely to transform others, for each language has its own structure, sounds, images and allusions. A few examples may help the reader to understand some of what is involved in the process of transformation when a poem is, as Adrienne Rich says, "rescored for a different instrument."

A first consideration is grammatical structure. Russian, for instance, has an elaborate system of participles which can be used as modifiers to suggest, let us say, different levels of penetration. It is impossible in English to say "the just-having-entered man," and the quality of such a careful distinction must change along with its grammatical form. And what of the expressions we use for the most ordinary things? The French term for "hobby" is *violon d'Ingres,* referring to the violin that the painter Ingres played in his spare time. This expression is meaningless in English and so its associations are lost in translation. Indeed, the vivid history of a culture may be contained in allusions. A striking case is modern Hebrew, which is seeded with Biblical references kept almost wholly intact during the two thousand years when the language was spoken chiefly for ritual purposes.

A matter of particular concern for translators of poetry is prosody, the metrical forms of verse which differ in use from one language to another. Verse translation always reflects or at least invokes the evolution of poetry in its own language. English and American poetry in the last twenty years has become characteristically spare, even conversational. On the other hand, the intricate prosody and rhyme patterns of traditional Russian verse have been preserved by contemporary Russian poets. The translator who attempts to reproduce the heavily rhymed songlike quality of Akhmatova's poetry in English, however, may easily turn out something that sounds to us more like a music hall ballad than like highly wrought verse.

The translators of the following poems have been aware of these considerations. Most have chosen, as Adrienne Rich suggests, to preserve the poetic image of the original poem within a clear and natural English. We hope that through these translations the reader will come close to each poet's "concrete and visionary apprehension of things in the world."

The Other Voice

Introduction

Recently people have been reading the work of women poets in English with intense and growing interest. University programs in women's studies, and the publication of new anthologies, have helped focus attention on this work. A large, long-neglected body of poetry with new themes and new concerns is beginning to receive the recognition it deserves.

Yet there remains a much larger body of poetry by women which is still unknown in this country: the poetry by women from non–English-speaking cultures. Except for the work of a few prominent figures such as Nelly Sachs, Gabriela Mistral, and Anna Akhmatova, this poetry is almost entirely unavailable. Most of it has never been translated into English. Foreign literature has until recently been largely identified with the European cultural centers, France and Germany. Translators have worked in a narrow range of less familiar languages. And when they do turn to poets writing in so-called exotic languages—as when the Imagists introduced Chinese poetry—they usually overlook the women. The selection of poems in this book, representing thirty-eight countries and thirty-one languages, is meant to show that women all over the world have written and are writing poetry of an extraordinary quality and importance for us today. Though only a small sampling of their work, and not intended as a representative survey, we think the poems included here are a fair reflection of the concerns of women poets in our time.

Ultimately, we believe it is important to understand the women poets within the contexts of their respective histories and traditions. At present, with the work of discovery hardly begun, this is only occasionally possible. Therefore we have chosen not to stress distinctions of time and place, but rather to arrange our selection according to recurrent themes that cut across cultural, geographical, and temporal boundaries. Our thematic divisions are purposely broad, to allow for a wide range of individual interpretations. And within each section the poems are placed so that each might benefit from the interplay of echoing and contrasting voices. A group of notes, beginning on page 195, glosses some possibly obscure allusions and references. Capsule biographies and bibliographies follow the notes.

The opening section, "Being a Woman," includes poems about the cultural and biological experience of womanhood. In Else Lasker-Schüler's "The Voices of Eden" Eve is invoked as the "seductress" who "seized the day from God," a female Prometheus offering a heroic, not a shameful, mythic model. The search for identity in figures of myth and legend is also reflected in "Sonnet to Eurydice" by Sophia de Mello Breyner Andresen and in Anne Hébert's "Eve." The question of identity is further explored in a number of self-portraits and portraits, such as Leah Goldberg's "On Myself 1" and Tove Ditlevsen's "Self Portrait 1" and "Self Portrait 2." Dahlia Ravikovitch's "Clockwork Doll" and Forūgh Farrokhzād's "Mechanical Doll"—each in a different way—represent woman as object through images of passivity, emptiness, and dismemberment. "Being a Woman" also contains a group of poems, including several from the oral poetry of traditional cultures, celebrating women's *rites de passage:* puberty, pregnancy, childbirth, old age. From a different perspective the Yiddish poets Kadia Molodowsky and Anna Margolin speak of the difficulty of escaping old models of womanhood and the need to find new concepts of self. Marina Tsvetayeva, in the last poem in this section, speaks of the price but also the glory of rebellion: "We shall not escape Hell, my passionate/sisters . . . we have been/the queens of the whole world!/ . . . we have/bartered away heaven,/in starry nights, in the apple/orchards of Paradise."

The poems in "Women and Men" explore different aspects of relationship—fulfillment in love, the desire for independence, and the anguish of conflict and separation. Again and again these poems return to the question of identity, the difficulty of defining oneself as a woman. The first poem in this sequence, "A Love Song," by Else Lasker-Schüler, is a poem of sexual desire. Maria Teresa Horta's erotic poem "Secret" is an even more direct assertion of female sexuality: "Don't tell them about my/skein/or my spinning wheel/nor what I do/with them/to hear you scream." In Tsvetayeva's "Poem of the End" the lovers' intense closeness threatens to destroy the woman's ability to act independently; the poem speaks of the awareness that too great an intimacy can lead to loss of self. There are also poems of tension and of bitter conflict. The angry voice of the wife-servant speaks in Sonja Åkesson's "The Marital Problem"—"Wife wash sauce/Wife cook dirt/Wife do dregs/ . . . Come crawling knees/begging/be White Man's slave." Often the struggle between men and women is the subject of wry, biting humor, as in Sarah Kirsch's "Brief Landing," in which the poet returns to his wife at Christmas-time only to pick a quarrel and depart when the holiday is over. In a more sober tone, in Tove Ditlevsen's "Divorce 1," the conventions of separation are satirized: "He would/in the case of a divorce/demand half/of everything/ . . . Half a sofa/ . . . half a pound of butter/half a child." Closing this section are two poems composed to be sung—"Goddam the Empty Sky," by Chilean folk-singer Violeta Parra, and "The Abandoned," by the North African Berber poet-singer Mririda n'Ait Attik—two very different responses to the experience of separation.

"Meditations" contains poems in which states of feeling are projected through images of nature and the cycle of seasonal change. These are poems of solitude, often of sadness. Many convey a sense of time passing, or of a time suspended, in which nothing comes to fruition. In "Dark Stream" Ingrid Jonker writes of the fear of life's secrets and of the risk of engulfment. In Malka Heifetz Tussman's "Water Without Sound" the still water of the canal becomes a metaphor for female stasis and silence, while in "Landscape," by Anne Hébert, the water is a marsh "Haunted by the hoarse cry/Of imaginary birds . . ."—an image of the decay of memory and the loss of childhood. Several poems, including Heifetz Tussman's "Spoil" and Majken Johansson's "Proportion Poetry," are explicitly about the difficulty of writing poetry, the infrequency of inspiration and the obstacles to concentration presented by daily life. Also in this section is the voice of tolerant, wise humor, as in Isabelle Vuckovic's "Maturity" and Dahlia Ravikovitch's "Pride."

In "Speaking for Others," "Requiem 1935–1940," written by Anna Akhmatova during the Stalinist purges and the Second World War, affirms her determination to survive personal grief and give voice to the suffering of others. Several poets speak out of their direct experience of struggle aginst repressive regimes. The Vietnamese poet Hien Luong in "Songs That Cannot Be Silenced" celebrates resistance to physical torture—"such power in frail bodies." In "Far from the Beach," by Alda do Espírito Santo, the figure of the mother becomes an image of dignity and strength in the midst of poverty. Another African poet, Noémia da Sousa, from Mozambique, raises a call to revolt: "Our voice lifts/over the white selfishness of men/ . . . a/summoning drumbeat." "The Marina Poems," by Lucha Corpi, are written in defense of a historical figure—Marina, or Malinche, the Indian woman taken as a mistress by Cortéz during the conquest of Mexico and considered by many as a traitor to her people.

The final group of poems is entitled "Visions." These are poems of revelation and metamorphosis. Simone Weil's "Random Thoughts on the Love of God" and Ping-hsin's "Receiving Buddha" are the only overtly religious poems in this group, and each is distinctive in its sense of the individual's relationship to God. Else Lasker-Schüler in "The Shulamite" speaks in the voice of the bride of *The Song of Songs,* according to mystical interpretation, Israel giving herself to her divine lover: "O, how your life beckons me!/And I vanish/With flowering heartache,/I blow away into space." In an entirely different kind of poem, "Cambrian, A Suite About the Sea and the Animals" Eeva-Liisa Manner envisions a prehistoric landscape in which birds, crocodiles, and shellfish are sunk in an instinctual stupor. They are "crawling souls/with their sucking mouths and groping brains." Yet even on this primitive level there is movement, change, the possibility of evolution. Several poets in this section, including Katerina Anghelaki-Rooke in "Diogenes" and Ágnes Nemes Nagy in "Ikhnaton's Night" project themselves into historical figures, embellished by legend, who staked their personal fates on heterodox views of the world. In the final poem of the anthology, Nemes Nagy, like Simone Weil in "Illuminations," suggests the possibility of the rebirth of self and of society, though the vision is seen through a mesh of ambiguity and doubt. After war and an avalanche of violent destruction, the mythical Ikhnaton picks himself up from the rubble and debris: "Between the long ribbons of fog/he went leading himself/left hand held in his right."

Being
a
Woman

Anne Hébert
Canada (*b. 1916*)

Eve

Queen, mistress, crucified at the gates of the furthest city

Red-plumed screech owl, wings nailed, all joints
disjointed, all wing-breadth fastened

Flesh, green apple acid, beautiful, wet orchard, I see you
wrecked, whipped by wind like a torn flag

Sharp, prying nose, hooked beak—these are our charms
against the day of plague

Your feathers and sifted bones will mantle us against
death and anger

Reclining woman, great anthill under the larch tree,
ancient land riddled with lovers

We invoke you, first womb, fine face of dawn lifting
through man's ribs the hard barrier of day

Your sons and husbands, see them rotting, swarming
between your legs under a single curse

Mother of Christ, remember your last born daughters, the
ones crushed, suddenly, between huge stones,
nameless and without history

Spring of tears and cries, the honor and weight of what
bright finery you leave us—anguish, love, joy,

celebrated at one table, etched in our features like a
 landscape

Blind mother, tell us of birth and death and the bold path
 between harsh shadows, world's poles, day's axes

And of the evil of the tree and its curved boughs in the
 garden, and of God, naked and clear, and of the sin
 you wanted so much, like shade at noon

Tell us of perfect love and of the first man defeated in your
 arms

Remember the first heart under the rites of morning, Eve,
 renew our face like a destiny soothed

War unfurls dreaded paths—horror, death join hands,
 united by identical secrets, the four elements,
 maelstrom, rising like offended savage gods

Under iron, flame licks gentleness clean to bone-white, its
 cry stabs innocence and guilt with one blade

Eve, look at us, know us, hold us with your eyes that have
 no pupils, consider how our hands adventure,
 spinning the mystery like coarse wool by night

The child at the breast makes a dove-like sound, man
 smells the odor of burnt bread and the middle of day
 folds over us like seamless water

Eve, we call you from the depths of sudden peace, as if our
 justified hearts could easily be our stay

May your memory burst in the sun and, at the risk of
   waking the crime, find the shadow of grace on your
   face like a black shaft of light

Translated from the French by Kathleen Weaver

Leah Goldberg
Israel   (1911–1970)

On Myself I

My time is carved in my poems
like the years of a tree in its rings
like the years of my life in my wrinkles.

I have no hard words—
no valves of hallucination.
My images are
transparent like church windows
through which
one can see
the changing light in the sky
and the falling
like dead birds
of my loves.

Translated from the Hebrew by Robert Alter

Anna Rydstedt-Dannstedt
Sweden (*b. 1928*)

This Thing Only

Where have you soared so still tonight?
Of tea vapour your wings are fragrant, my soul
My tongue tastes lemon
but darkness is still your air, my soul.

Yet I see people
women and men at the tables in Europe
I too am born and
grown to be this thing only:
to be Anna in the world.

Translated from the Swedish by Joanna Bankier

Sophia de Mello Breyner Andresen
Portugal   (b. 1919)

Sonnet to Eurydice

Lost Eurydice who in the odours
And voices of ocean is seeking Orpheus
Absence that peoples land and sky
And muffles the whole world with silence

Thus I gulped the mists of morning
And renounced life and identity
In search of a face that was mine
My own face, secret and authentic

But neither in tides nor illusions
Did I find you. Only the smooth pure face
Of the landscape rose before me

And slowly I became transparent
A dead woman burgeoning in your likeness
But lost in this world, and barren.

Translated from the Portuguese by Ruth Fainlight

Julia de Burgos
Puerto Rico *(1914–1953)*

To Julia de Burgos

The word is out that I am your enemy
   that in my poetry I am giving you away.

They lie, Julia de Burgos. They lie, Julia de Burgos.
That voice that rises in my poems is not yours: it is my
     voice;
you are the covering and I the essence;
and between us lies the deepest chasm.

You are the frigid doll of social falsehood,
and I, the virile sparkle of human truth.

You are honey of courtly hypocrisy, not I;
I bare my heart in all my poems.

You are selfish, like your world, not I;
I gamble everything to be what I am.

You are but the grave lady, ladylike;
not I; I am life, and strength, and I am woman.

You belong to your husband, your master, not I;
I belong to no one or to everyone, because to all, to all
I give myself in pure feelings and in my thoughts.

You curl your hair, and paint your face, not I;
I am curled by the wind, painted by the sun.

You are lady of the house, resigned and meek,
tied to the prejudices of men, not I;
I am Rocinante, running headlong,
smelling the horizons of the justice of God.

Translated from the Spanish by María Arrillaga

Gloria Fuertes
Spain (*b. 1918*)

I've Never Got Anything

I've never got anything in my gray purse,
never anything to dress up in,
always the same shoes without laces,
the same black shag to smoke, and I don't care.

There's a crystal nailed under my tongue
and a new being . . . Look, I'm going to talk about a new
     being.

What old idiot cried that there were no souls left?
I just met one with a halo and all
who said I was OK, so I throw myself down
and beat the earth with my open fists.

All of a sudden my sad purse filled,
my hair straightened and my looks shaped up.
To hell with these shoes with their tongues hanging out,
today a new bird sings in my cage.

Now

Now I'm going to tell you
how the worms
I fed on mulberry leaves
in an empty soap carton
changed themselves
into great fluffs of color,

and how later I saw them
transported into butterflies,
and all this because it was May
and insects are, in their way, magicians.

Then I'll tell you
how Eloise Muro,
the fourth mistress of Cervantes,
wrote *Don Quijote*.

Because though tiny, I know many things,
and my body is an endless eye
through which, unfortunately, I see everything.

Translated from the Spanish by Philip Levine

Kadia Molodowsky
United States (*Yiddish*)   (*b. 1894*)

Women Songs I

The faces of women long dead, of our family,
come back in the night, come in dreams to me saying:
We have kept our blood pure through long generations,
we brought it to you like a sacred wine
from the kosher cellars of our hearts.
And one of them whispers:
I remained deserted, when my two rosy apples
still hung on the tree
and I gritted away the long nights of waking between my
   white teeth.

I will go to meet the grandmothers, saying:
Your sighs were the whips that lashed me
and drove my young life to the threshold
to escape from your kosher beds.
But wherever the street grows dark you pursue me—
wherever a shadow falls.

Your whimperings race like the autumn wind past me,
and your words are the silken cord
still binding my thoughts.
My life is a page ripped out of a holy book
and part of the first line is missing.

      Translated from the Yiddish by Adrienne Rich

Anna Margolin
United States (Yiddish) *(1887–1952)*

Years

Women much loved, who never had enough,
going through life with laughter and anger,
their eyes brilliant as fires or agates—
that's how the years were.

And they were actors playing Hamlet,
muttering disdainfully with half a mouth;
arrogant tyrants of a rebellious state
dashing the rebels down.

Yet see how dispirited they are now,
my God! dumb as a smashed keyboard
they quiver at every threat or jeer,
searching for you, in whom they don't believe.

Translated from the Yiddish by Adrienne Rich

Alfonsina Storni
Argentina *(1892–1938)*

It May Be

Maybe all that my verses have expressed
is simply what was never allowed to be;
only what was hidden and suppressed
from woman to woman, from family to family.

They say that in my house tradition was
the rule by which one did things properly;
they say the women of my mother's house
were always silent—yes, it well may be.

Sometimes my mother felt longings to be free,
but then a bitter wave rose to her eyes
and in the shadows she wept.
And all this—caustic, betrayed, chastised—
all this that in her soul she tightly kept,
I think that, without knowing, I have set it free.

Translated from the Spanish by Mark I. Smith

Forūgh Farrokhzād
Iran   *(1935–1967)*

A Window

One window for seeing
one window for hearing
one window that reaches like a well shaft
deep into the heart of the earth—
And onto this expanse of blue and recurring kindness
opens a window
for the night fragrance of stars
pouring into hands small with loneliness,
for the sun persuaded to visit
homesick geraniums—
One window is all I need

I come from the country of dolls
from the shade of paper trees
in a picture-book garden
from dry seasons,
                fruitless trials of friendship and love
in the dusty roads of innocence—
from years of pallid letters, growing into an alphabet
behind the desks of consumptive schools
out of that instant when the children learned
to spell "stone" across the blackboard
and starlings scattered in alarm from the old tree

I come from among the roots of carnivorous plants,
and my head still rings
with a butterfly's cry of terror
as it's pinned in a notebook
When all my trust dangled from the weak thread of justice
and all through the city

they went smashing my heart-lamps,
when they bound my childish eyes of love
with the thick blindfold of the law
and the throbbing temples of my longing
streamed fountains of blood,
when my life was nothing more
nothing at all but the tick-tocking of a clock on the wall—
then I knew I must
I must
I must
crazily love

One window is all I need
one window onto a moment of consciousness, seeing, and
        silence
By now the walnut sapling
is tall enough to interpret the wall
to its unfolding leaves
Ask the mirror
the name of your savior
Isn't the earth rotting beneath your feet
more lonely than you?
The prophets have brought their message of doom
along with them down to our time
These explosions one after the other
these poisonous clouds
do they reverberate the Sacred Word?
Friend—brother—fellow-being
when you reach the moon
record the history of the genocide of flowers

Dreams always
fall from the height of their simplicity and die

I kiss the clover that grows
four-leafed from the grave of old ideas
The woman buried in the shroud of her own long-waiting
    chastity,
        was she my youth?
Will I climb again the stairs of my own curiosity
to greet the good Lord who walks about on the roof?

I sense that time has passed
I sense that this moment is my portion in the turning
    calendar
I sense that this table is a deceptive space between my
    hair
           and the hands of this sad stranger

Speak to me
speak to me
I give you the tenderness of a living body
all I ask is awareness of the touch of life

Speak to me—
I stand here in the window
warmed by the sun

Translated from the Persian by Deirdre Lashgari

Venus Khoury
Lebanon (*b. 1937*)

My father has big skin like a soldier's cape
My father has a huge chest like a sailboat
My father is the ocean.

My mother crushes the sand second by second
for the beads of gold that
my sisters with faded, sticky eyes
find, then string together in
fugitive suns.

Translated from the French by Carol Cosman

Blaga Dmitrova
Bulgaria   (b. 1922)

To My Father

You gathered incredible strength
in order to die
to seem calm and fully conscious
without complaint, without trembling
without a cry
so that I would not be afraid

Your wary hand
slowly grew cold in mine
and guided me carefully
beyond into the house of death
so I might come to know it

Thus in the past you used to take my hand
and guide me through the world
and show me life
so I would not fear

I will follow after you
confident as a child
toward the silent country
where you went first
so I would not feel a stranger there

And I will not be afraid.

Translated from the Bulgarian into French by J. Bossolova
and Guillevic. English version by Joanna Bankier.

Ingrid Jonker
South Africa *(1933–1965)*

Ladybird (a memory of my mother)

Gleam ochre
and a light breaks
out of the sea.
In the backyard
somewhere among the washing
and a tree full of pomegranates
your laugh in the morning
sudden and small
is like a ladybird
fallen on my hand

Translated from the Africaans by Jack Cope and
William Plomer

Tove Ditlevsen
Denmark (*b. 1918*)

Self Portrait   I

I can not:
cook
wear a hat
make people comfortable
wear jewelry
arrange flowers
remember appointments
thank others for gifts
tip correctly
keep a man
show interest
at meetings for parents.

I can not
stop:
smoking
drinking
eating chocolate
stealing umbrellas
oversleeping
forgetting to remember
birthdays
and to clean my nails.
Telling people
what they want to hear
giving away secrets
liking
strange places
and psychopaths.

I can:
be alone
wash dishes
read books
form sentences
listen
and be happy
without guilt.

Self Portrait   2

When you have
once had
a great joy
it lasts always
quivers gently
on the edge of all the
insecure adult days
subdues inherited dread
makes sleep deeper.

The bedroom was
an island of light
my father and mother
were painted
on the morning's wall.
They handed a shining
picture book toward me
they smiled to see
my immense joy.

I saw they were young
and happy for
each other
saw it for the first
saw it for the last time.

The world became eternally
divided into a before
and after.
I was five years old
since then everything
has changed.

Translated from the Danish by Ann Freeman

Forūgh Farrokhzād
Iran *(1935–1967)*

Mechanical Doll

Oh yes, even more than this
more than this you can keep silent

You can stare
for hours at the smoke of a cigarette
stare at the outline of a cup
at a faded flower in the carpet
at an imagined line upon the wall,
with fixed eyes, like the eyes of the dead
You can draw aside the curtain
with stiffened fingers, and watch
a heavy rain falling in the alley
a child in a doorway
clutching his painted kite
a worn-out cart clattering off
from the empty square

You can be left there standing
by the curtain, blind and deaf

You can cry out
in a voice so false, so strange
"I love—"
Can offer to the powerful arms of a man
a body like a chamois spread,
the firm big breasts
of a clean, attractive female
You can

in the bed of some drunk, some tramp, some fool
defile the chastity of a love

You can so cleverly reduce to nothing
any strange and wondrous riddle
Can sit alone over a crossword puzzle
can busy yourself with some meaningless answer
a pointless answer, yes, in five or six letters

You can kneel for a lifetime
with bowed head, at the foot of a cold tomb
can see God over some stranger's grave
can find faith in a handful of coins
can rot in the cubicles of a mosque
like some old reader of pilgrims' prayers

You can, like zero in addition or subtraction
always end up with the same result
can watch your eyes, in the hard cocoon of their anger
become blank eyelets of a worn-out shoe
can, like water, dry up in your own ditch

You can conceal a moment's beauty
—like some awful instant photo—
shamefully, in the bottom of a drawer
Can hang within the empty frame of a day
some face condemned, or crucified, or crushed
You can cover the crack across the wall with masks
you can dissolve in images yet more absurd

You can be a wind-up doll
and view your world with two glass eyes—

You can sleep in a cloth-lined box
for years among the net and spangles,
your body stuffed with straw,
can with every pressure of a greasy hand
give a cry
"Oh how lucky I am!"

Translated from the Persian by Deirdre Lashgari

Dahlia Ravikovitch
Israel (*b. 1936*)

Portrait

She sits in the house for days on end.
She reads the papers.
(What's the matter, don't you?)
She doesn't do what she'd like to do,
things get in the way.
She wants vanilla, lots of vanilla,
give her vanilla.

In winter she's cold, really cold,
colder than other people.
She bundles up but she's still cold.
She wants vanilla.

She wasn't born yesterday, if that's
what you're thinking.
This isn't the first time she's felt the cold.
Not the first time it's winter.
In fact summer isn't so pleasant either.
She reads the paper more than she'd like to.
In winter she won't budge without the heater.
Sometimes she gets fed up.
Did she ever ask you for much?
You'll admit she hasn't.
She wants vanilla.

If you'll look closely, she's
got a tartan skirt.
She likes a tartan skirt because it's sporty.
Just to look at her, you'd laugh.
It's all so ludicrous.

Even she laughs about it sometimes.
She has a hard time in winter,
a rough time in summer,
you'd laugh.
Call her mimosa,
a bird without wings,
call her whatever you like.
She's always wrapping herself up in something
and stifling,
sometimes a tartan skirt and other stuff.
Why wrap herself up if it's stifling?
These things are complicated.
It's the cold in winter, the impossible
heat in summer,
never the way you want it.
And by the way, don't forget,
she wants vanilla.
Now she's even crying.
Give her vanilla.

Translated from the Hebrew by Chana Bloch

Nuala ní Dhomhnaill
Ireland   (b. 1952)

Móir Hatching

I'm telling you,
stubborn Móir,
that green snakes will come
from your womb
if you stay sitting
on festering knowledge
one day longer.

Gather into yourself
like a bee
the hours that fall open
under the bright shaft of the sun
ripening in heat,
store them
and make of them
           honey days.

Translated from the Gaelic by Joan Keefe

Nina Cassian
Romania (*b. 1924*)

The Kiwi Bird

(*A bird in New Zealand
that's forgotten how to fly*)

I am the Kiwi bird
the one without wings . . .
Don't speak to me.
Don't call me.
I don't understand you . . .
Because I can't fly
and because some children
throw stones at me
I've become dull.
My beak opens sometimes, by itself
as if I were thirsty,
as if I were sick,
but I'm neither thirsty nor sick,
I am only dull
very, very dull.
Other times however,
I think I hear something,
something like a flapping of sheets in the wind,
of wings in flight,
and then I walk a little,
I raise my stiff legs,
and my steps seem suddenly alert—
but I immediately sit down on the ground
and with my long beak,
I begin to scratch my wingless back
as if there were nothing left in the world
but me and my beak that pokes.
I am the Kiwi bird, the one that can't comprehend.

Don't speak to me.
Don't call me.
Once every few years, it happens,
when the moon seems to hum, to ring in a certain way
that shame and sorrow, my only emotions
start glimmering in my flesh,
and then I want to hide
and I have nowhere,
and I bend and twist,
and I have nothing with which to cover myself.

I am the Kiwi bird
the one without wings.
I am the Kiwi bird.

Translated from the Romanian by Laura Schiff

Karin Boye
Sweden (*1900–1941*)

A Sword

A sword
flexible, supple and strong
a dancing sword
proudly obeying the stern laws
the hard rhythms in the steel.
A sword
I wanted to be—soul and body.

I hate
this wretched willow soul of mine,
patiently enduring, plaited or twisted
by other hands.
I hate you
my lazy, dreamy soul.
You shall die.
Help me, my hate, sister of my longing
Help me be
a sword,
a dancing sword of tempered steel.

Translated from the Swedish by Joanna Bankier

Anonymous
Papago, North American Indian

Song for a Young Girl's Puberty Ceremony

I am on my way running,
I am on my way running,
Looking toward me is the edge of the world,
I am trying to reach it,
The edge of the world does not look far away,
To that I am on my way running.

Translated from the Papago by Frances Densmore

Anonymous
New Guinea

Song for a Girl
on Her First Menstruation

Hold, hold it tight,
grasp the black crayfish,
hold, hold it tight.
Grab the white eel,
Sisirik, Miampa lumbo
grasp the black crayfish
Kayame Parilumpo
kill the white eel.

Translated from the Boikin by Joe Prentuo

Ingrid Jonker
South Africa *(1933–1965)*

Pregnant Woman

I lie under the crust of the night singing,
curled up in the sewer, singing,
and my bloodchild lies in the water.

I play that I'm a child:
gooseberries, gooseberries and heather,
kukumakrankas, anise,
and the tadpole glides
in the slime in the stream
in my body
my foam-white image;
but sewer O sewer
my bloodchild lies in the water.

Still singing flesh-red our blood-song,
I and my yesterday,
my yesterday hangs under my heart,
my wild lily, my lullaby world,
and my heart that sings like a cicada,
my cicada-heart sings like a cicada;
but sewer O sewer,
my bloodchild lies in the water.

I play that I'm happy:
look where the firefly sparkles!
the moon-disc, a wet snout that quivers—
but with the morning, the limping midwife,
grey and shivering on the sliding hills,
I push you out through the crust into daylight,
O sorrowing owl, great owl of the daylight

free from my womb but besmeared,
with my tears all smeared
and tainted with grief.

Sewer O sewer
I lie trembling, singing,
how else but trembling
with my bloodchild under your water . . . ?

Translated from the Afrikaans by Jack Cope and
William Plomer

Anonymous
Papago, North American Indian

Song of a woman in labor

towering rocks
sound
in the evening
with them
I cry

Translated from the Papago by Frances Densmore
Adapted by Kathleen Weaver

Anonymous

Seminole, North American Indian

Song for Bringing a Child into the World

You day-sun, circling around,
You daylight, circling around,
You night-sun, circling around,
You poor body, circling around,
You wrinkled age, circling around,
You spotted with gray, circling around,
You wrinkled skin, circling around.

Translated from the Seminole by Frances Densmore

Anonymous
Ten'a, Alaskan Indian

the choice

while she was berrying
she bore that child
laid it on grass
and berried some more
she came back, creeping

she came back, creeping
and sprang forward
screaming
to terrify that child
then she left

she came back, creeping
and did those things again
once twice three times
the fourth time the child
changed it was a bird
flew away

*Translated from the Ten'a by John W. Chapman. English
version by Armand Schwerner.*

Máire Mhac an tSaoi
Ireland (*b. 1922*)

The First Shoe

We put the shoe on him the first time this morning,
minute, stitched-together, a little jewel of leather,
a miracle of shoemaking, in the first choice of fashion,
on the flowerlike foot never before in bondage,
the first shoe ever on that small honey-sweet foot.

Little treasure, heart of the house, here you go tramping,
strike the sole like this on the ground stoutly,
hold the precious head pluckily, determined,
a man-baby you are in your walk and your bearing,
the height of my knee, and so soon to leave me!

You have a long road to travel before you,
and tying your shoe is only the first tying.

Translated from the Gaelic by Brendan O Hehir

Ana Blandiana
Romania (b. 1943)

I Have the Right

Do I have the right to end
The line started at the world's beginning
Or maybe earlier
From the amoeba-God
Torn in two,
Beamed through fishes, flown through birds
Reaching my ancestors?
Do I have the right to answer suddenly
No
To the long line of suffering through which
I've been killed from parent to parent
To myself?
Can I return
In death among them
And tell them
That I left no one in my place?
Oh, yes,
How could I thank them
Any other way
For the stillness that awaits me
Than by bringing them the final stillness
By telling them: "It's over,
My parents, my guardians
Nothing binds you
To life,
You are free!"
And with the gentle gesture with
Which children pet their parents
I'd tie this death halo around their forehead
And move them smiling among saints.

Translated from the Romanian by Laura Schiff

Cecília Meireles
Brazil *(1901–1967)*

Ballad of the
Ten Casino Dancers

Ten dancers glide
across a mirror floor.
They have thin gilt plaques on Egyptian bodies,
fingertips reddened, blue lids painted,
lift white veils naively scented,
bend yellow knees.

The ten dancers go
voiceless among customers,
hands above knives, teeth above roses,
little lamps befuddled by cigars.
Between the music and the movement flows
depravity, a flight of silken stairs.

The dancers now advance
like ten lost grasshoppers,
advance, recoil, avoiding glances
in the close room, and plucking at the din
they are so naked, you imagine
them clothed in the stuff of tears.

The ten dancers screen
their pupils under great green lashes.
Death passes tranquil as a belt around
their phosphorescent waists.
As who should bear a dead child to the ground
each bears her flesh that moves and scintillates.

Fat men watch in massive tedium
those cold, cold dancers,
pitiful serpents without appetite
who are children by daylight.
Ten anemic angels made of hollows,
melancholy embalms them.

Ten mummies in a band,
back and forth go the tired dancers.
Branch whose fragrant blossoms bend
blue, green, gold, white.
Ten mothers would weep at the sight
of those dancers hand in hand.

Translated from the Portuguese by James Merrill

Dahlia Ravikovitch

Israel (*b. 1936*)

Clockwork Doll

That night, I was a clockwork doll,
And I turned all around, to the left and the right,
And I fell on my face and shattered to bits,
And they tried to patch me with all of their skill.

And once again, I was a proper doll,
My manner carefully poised and polite.
But then I was a doll of a different sort,
A broken twig that only a tendril holds.

And then I went out to dance at the ball,
But they left me with a rabble of dogs and cats
Though all my steps were measured and rhythmical.

And I had blue eyes and I had golden hair
And I had a dress the color of garden flowers
And I had a trimming of cherries on my straw hat.

Translated from the Hebrew by Chana Bloch

Anonymous
Eskimo, Greenland

song of the old woman

all these heads these ears these eyes
around me
how long will the ears hear me?
and those eyes how long
will they look at me?
when these ears won't hear me any more
when these eyes turn aside from my eyes
I'll eat no more raw liver with fat
and those eyes won't see me any more
and my hair my hair will have disappeared

Translated from the Eskimo into French by Paul-Emile
Victor. English version by Armand Schwerner.

Else Lasker-Schüler
Germany (*1869–1945*)

The Voices of Eden

More wild, more rash, Eve, admit it
your longing was the snake,
its voice curled over your lip
bit into the edge of your cheek.

More wild, more fierce, Eve, admit it
you seized the day from God
you took your dawn too early
and sunk into shame's blind well.

Then, stirring suddenly,
immense, first timid like
fulfillment,
out of your womb, self-creating—
the God-like soul . . .

And it grows over the world
and all of time,
losing its beginnings,
and back round your myriad heart
without end.

Sing, Eve, your scared lonely song,
lonelier, drop-heavy like your beating heart,
unbind the gloomy chain of tears
that winds round the world's neck.

Like moonlight, change your aspect,
you are lovely . . .

sing, sing, listen—the rustling note
the night plays, knowing nothing of what occurred.

Everywhere the deaf din—
your fear rolls over the steps of earth
down the back of God.

There's hardly a handspan between Him and you.
Hide deep in the eye of night,
let your day wear night-darkness.

Heaven chokes, bending down after stars—
shepherdess Eve, the blue doves
are moaning in Eden.

Eve, turn round at the last hedge!
Cast no shadow with you.
Flower fully, seductress!

Eve, you ardent listener,
O you foamwhite cluster,
flee even your eyelashes'
fine cutting edge.

Translated from the German by Robert Alter

Marina Tsvetayeva
Soviet Union *(1894–1941)*

We Shall Not Escape Hell

We shall not escape Hell, my passionate
sisters, we shall drink black resins—
we who sang our praises to the Lord
with every one of our sinews, even the finest,

we did not lean over cradles or
spinning wheels at night, and now we are
carried off by an unsteady boat
under the skirts of a sleeveless cloak,

we dressed every morning in
fine Chinese silk, and we would
sing our paradisal songs at
the fire of the robbers' camp,

slovenly needlewomen (all
our sewing came apart), dancers,
players upon pipes: we have been
the queens of the whole world!

first scarcely covered by rags,
then with constellations in our hair, in
gaol and at feasts we have
bartered away heaven,

in starry nights, in the apple
orchards of Paradise.
—Gentle girls, my beloved sisters,
we shall certainly find ourselves in Hell!

Translated from the Russian by Elaine Feinstein

*Women
and
Men*

Else Lasker-Schüler
Germany   *(1869–1945)*

A Love Song

Come to me in the night—let us sleep entwined.
I am so tired, and lonely from waking.
In the dawndark an alien bird has just sung
While my dream still wrestled with itself and me.

Blossoms open by every spring,
Taking on the strawflower color of your eyes . . .

Come to me in the night on seven-star-shoes,
Wrapped in love come late to my tent.
Moons rise from the dusty chests of the sky.

We shall rest from love like two rare beasts
In the high reeds behind this world.

Translated from the German by Robert Alter

Ann Smith

Sweden (*b. 1930*)

Desire makes you
beautiful
the field of your face
filled
brinkful
with streaming myrrh

You are beautiful when
you receive
like
a child

You are
beautiful your arms
stretched out
as if
sunbathing

Then I will stream over you
myrrh
and spiral
reach all cavities
reach all
mouths
all
open
wells

Translated from the Swedish by Joanna Bankier

Nadia Tuéni
Lebanon (*b. 1935*)

This evening
the night protecting me is lost in the city
the moon is a picture
This evening
a memory stubborn as a nettle
as daily bread
turns into a bird of passage on the walls
This evening there is room for everything that travels
colored boats line up in my eyes
a resonant world lives under the rain
your body is the rainbow before dawn
my voice turns around death
This evening
a Passion crosses the desert, led by a magus
your arms are sweet water
the night protecting me is closed around you

Translated from the French by Carol Cosman

Maria Teresa Horta
Portugal (*b. 1937*)

Secret

Don't tell them about my
dress
which I pull
over my head
nor that I drew
the curtains
to make the dark more dark

Let me close
the ring
around your neck
with my long
legs
and the shadow of my well

Don't tell them about my
skein
or my spinning wheel
nor what I do
with them
to hear you scream.

Translated from the Portuguese by Suzette Macedo

Marie Luise Kaschnitz
West Germany   (*b. 1901*)

from Return to Frankfurt

The girl thinks   if I can only manage
not to step on any of these
delicate hands of shadow
cast on the sidewalk by the chestnut trees

The boy thinks   if I reach the trolley
in time and if it doesn't have to wait
at the switch and the traffic policeman really
does his job and tries to clear the street

If   thinks the girl   before I reach that tree
the third on the left no nun comes out at me
and if not more than twice I pass small boys
crossing the street in groups, carrying toys
oh   then it's certain that we'll meet

Unless   the boy thinks   there's a power failure
unless forked lightning strikes the driver
unless the trolley-car gets smashed to bits
surely we'll meet   yes I can count on it

And many times the girl must shiver
And the boy think   will this last forever
until under the chestnut trees they meet,
wordless and smiling, in some quiet street.

Anonymous
Chippewa, North American Indian

Love Charm Songs

1
I can charm the man
He is completely fascinated by me

2
In the center of the earth
Wherever he may be
Or under the earth

My Love Has Departed

A loon
I thought it was
But it was
My love's
Splashing oar

Why Should I Be Jealous

Why should
I, even I
Be jealous
Because of that bad boy

When I Think of Him

Although he said it
Still
I am filled with longing
When I think of him

Translated from the Chippewa by Frances Densmore

Barbro Backberger
Sweden (*b. 1932*)

I'm Taking Off . . .

There is an aggressive ring at my door
There is a stirring nervousness in my room
It is him!

I'm taking off
I step over the windowsill
to hell with overpublicized men
and overdebated sexuality.

Calm as a witch at Easter
I am riding on the ridge of my brickgaudy roof
combing my hair over white cubebuildings
and gazing out over the glaring pink eveningsky.

Far far away in the evening of evenings
beyond the rounded horizon of the city
the skies are reflected
the heavens dive
the eveningglow drinks itself
drunk with morningglow
in Cambrian seas.

There a family of dinosaurs splashes
in a blankbown marsh
and mirrors the floating giant fern
in faithful charcoalgrey eyes.

It is early
it is before Man
it is before the ringcircuits of the nerves.

Translated from the Swedish by Joanna Bankier

Ingrid Jonker
South Africa *(1933–1965)*

Time of Waiting in Amsterdam

I can only say I have waited for you
through western nights
at bus stops
in lanes
by canals
on airfields
and the gallows of tears

And then you came
through the forlorn cities of Europe
I recognized you
I set out the table for you
with wine with bread with mercy
but imperturbably you turned your back
you detached your sex laid it down on the table
and without speaking a word
with your own smile
abandoned the world

*Translated from the Afrikaans by Jack Cope and William
Plomer*

Celia Dropkin
United States (Yiddish) (*1888–1956*)

Poem

You sowed in me, not a child
but yourself.
So it's you growing in me daily,
greater and more distinct.
There's no room left inside me
for myself
and my soul lies like a dog at your feet
growing fainter and fainter.
But, dying into you,
I still, even now, can make you songs.

Translated from the Yiddish by Adrienne Rich

Venus Khoury
Lebanon (*b. 1937*)

Our walls were thick
the wind sealed our doors with wandering sands
We were equal silences
Our eyes, simple ornaments, were noisy baubles
cheap jewels
I was called your wife
Our nights bore partings like
       convulsions
Dream-rides on horseback
broken by dawn
You talked about doors battered down single-handed
about a narrow bed thrown out like scrap iron

To be free, we must speak
Then we could share the stars without counting,
       without looking
The stars know each other
as we know great rivers on
their humble return from exile

Translated from the French by Carol Cosman

Venus Khoury
Lebanon (b. 1937)

Backed up against time
I put on my loveliest woman's skin to see you disappear
Twilight-pale
you call me brightness
like those days when the sea cleans its house of sand
when the sea heaves
You think those are seagulls
it's only the linen of the drowned
full of screams
I've torn myself from the lights to witness your eclipse
you call me your winter frost
your sweetness
when my breast is a bird of hot coals
when my flesh howls . . .

Translated from the French by Carol Cosman

Odette Aslan
France

I discover you in bits and pieces
I flay layered skins
scales dissolving in
the acid air.
I approach your truth
I reconstruct you—
calloused crust
shiny shell
green scum.
This debris torn out of you
isn't like you any more
I conjure you up and
you dissolve
bit by bit
in my fabulous alembic.

Translated from the French by Carol Cosman

Edith Södergran
Sweden (*1892–1923*)

Love

My soul of heaven's light blue
I left on a cliff by the sea.
Naked I came to you and resembled a woman
as a woman I sat at your table
and drank a cup of wine and inhaled the scent of roses.
You thought I was beautiful
                      like something seen in a dream

I forgot everything
I forgot my childhood and my country
I only knew your caresses held me prisoner.
Smiling, you took a mirror
and asked me to look at myself
I saw my shoulders were crumbling to dust
I saw my beauty was sickly and wished to be gone
Oh, hold me in your arms so tightly that I need nothing
    more.

        Translated from the Swedish by Joanna Bankier

Natalya Gorbanevskaya
Soviet Union (*b. 1936*)

And there is nothing at all—neither fear,
nor a stiffening before the executioner.
I lay my head upon the hollowed block,
as on a casual lover's shoulder.

Roll, curly head, over the planed boards,
mind you don't get a splinter in your parted lips—
the boards bruise your temples, the trumpets
sound solemnly in your ears;

the polished copper dazzles you,
the horses' manes toss,—
O, what a day to die on!

Another day dawns sunless,

And in the semidark—either
through sleepiness, some ancient madness,
or new apocrypha—my lover's shoulder
still smells to me of pine shavings.

Anonymous
Eskimo, Greenland

a woman's song, about men

first I lowered my head
and for a start I stared at the ground
for a second I couldn't say anything
but now that they're gone
I raise my head I look straight ahead I can answer
They say I stole a man
the husband of one of my aunts
they say I took him for a husband of my own
lies
fairy tales
slander
It was him, he
lay down next to me
But they're men
which is why they lie
that's the reason
and it's my hard luck.

*Translated from the Eskimo into French by Paul-Emile
Victor. English version by Armand Schwerner.*

Sarah Kirsch
East Germany (*b. 1935*)

Brief Landing

When it gets towards Christmas
the poets return
to their capable wives
Oh how they ran all year
all over the earth
the things they heard the
things they thought about! they
wrote their newspaper
climbed through factories
taught the potato
human forms of conduct
gazed at the smoke
creeping and rising
they swallowed everything, sometimes
Manhattan cocktails because of the
name, they sharpened the
class struggle, meditated
on the abstract in fish
until one day
there penetrates
through their thin coats the cold
a longing
for a real fish in a dish
suddenly overwhelms them
and the memory
of the wife who's warmed herself by the fire
they leave
their rags in the cities they come
with curious hats for their children
rinse out the washing even, play the piano, until,

after New Year's Eve, they've had enough they
pick a quarrel then and—relieved—depart
in the gloves from under the Christmas tree

Translated from the German by Gerda Mayer

Maria Banus
Romania (*b. 1914*)

Wedding

In the nuptial room there was a black, cosmic cold.

Undress, I told him, make me warm.

First he unscrewed his head, it grated like Saturn
trying to escape the vise of his rings,
or like the stopper of a bottle
when it shrieks against the glass throat.
He unscrewed his right arm
with its bullet threading.
He unscrewed his left arm
like a supple metallic rocket.
He unscrewed his artificial right leg,
swearing like a truck driver at a hacking engine.
He unscrewed his artificial left leg,
and iron groaned against iron,
like a boiler room.

I crawled near his heart,
I put my head on his chest,
I listened to the pulse of his heart.
It didn't grate, it didn't clank, it didn't explode—
it throbbed.

Blades of grass grew all around,
and a rabbit's face appeared among the hazel branches,
a sky, a milky streak of cloud.
Then, finally, I cried.

Translated from the Romanian by Laura Schiff

Marina Tsvetayeva
Soviet Union (*1892–1941*)

from Poem of the End

I

A single post, a point of rusting
    tin in the sky
marks the fated place we
    move to, he and I

on time   as death is
    prompt strangely
too smooth the gesture of
    his hat to me

menace at the edges of his
    eyes his mouth tight
shut   strangely too low is the
    bow he makes tonight

on time?   that false note in
    his voice, what
is it the brain alerts to and the
    heart drops at?

under that evil sky, that sign of
    tin and rust
Six o'clock.   There he is waiting
    by the post.

Now we kiss soundlessly, his
    lips stiff as
hands are given to queens, or
    dead people thus

round us the shoving elbows of
        ordinary bustle
and strangely irksome rises the
        screech of a whistle

howls like a dog screaming
        angrier, longer: what
a nightmare strangeness life is
        at death point

and that nightmare reached my waist
        only, last night
and now reaches the stars, it has
        grown to its true height

crying silently love love until
        —Has it gone
six, shall we go to the cinema?
        I shout it: home!

                    8
Last   bridge   I won't
give up or take out my hand
this is the last bridge
the last bridging between

water   and firm land:
and I am saving these
coins for death
for Charon, the price of Lethe

this   shadow money
from my dark hand I press
soundlessly into
the shadowy darkness of his

shadow money it is
no gleam and tinkle in it
coins for shadows:
the dead have enough poppies

This bridge

Lovers for the most
part are without hope: passion
also is just
a bridge, a means of connection

It's warm: to nestle
close at your ribs, to move in
a visionary pause
towards nothing, beside nothing

no   arms no   legs
now, only the bone of my
side is alive where
it presses directly against you

life in that side
only, ear and echo is it: there
I stick like white to
egg yolk, or an Eskimo to his fur

adhesive, pressing
joined to you: Siamese

twins are no nearer.
The woman you call mother

when she forgot
all things in motionless triumph
only to carry you:
she did not hold you closer.

Understand: we have
grown into one as we slept and
now I can't jump
because I can't let go your hand

and I won't be torn off
as I press close to you: this
bridge is no husband
but a lover: a just slipping past

our support: for the
river is fed with bodies!
I bite in like a tick
you must tear out my roots to be rid of me

like ivy   like a tick
inhuman   godless
to throw me away like a
thing, when there is

no thing I ever prized
in this empty world of things
Say this is only dream,
night still and afterwards morning

an express   to Rome?
Granada?   I won't know myself

as I push off
the Himalayas of bedclothes

But this dark is deep:
now I warm you with my blood, listen
to this flesh.
It is far truer than poems

If you are warm, who
will you go to tomorrow for that?
This is delirium,
please say this bridge cannot

end
        as it ends.

Translated from the Russian by Elaine Feinstein

Anne Hébert
Canada   (*b. 1916*)

Wisdom Has Broken My Arms

Wisdom has broken my arms, shattered my bones—
An envious woman, very old,
Pious, full of gall and green water

She threw her sweetness in my face
Wanting to dissolve my features like a wet image
Smoothing my anger like drowned hair

And I cried out under the bland insult
And I took back the iron and fire of my heritage.

Wanting to plant her soul there, blessed like a vine,
She carved out a place between my ribs.
For ages her perfume poisoned me from head to toe.

But the storm was ripening under my arms,
Musk, burnt leaves,
I tore out wisdom from my breast,
I ate it by the roots,
Found it bitter and spat it out like a rotten pit

I remembered my cruellest friend, exiled by the city,
          hands full of stones.
I went with him to die on ripe beaches
O my love, prepare the glint of your heart, we will
          battle until dawn
Violence hurls us up in towering forests
Our riches are deep and black like ore in mines
          where lightning strikes

En route, it is day, fever deep in the sealed heart
Cock cries break through the night like flares
The sun barely risen, already sure of noon
Fire, arrows, desire, in the strongest light
One way or another, all life in a single honor.

Hard, unshaded paths open as far as the eye can see
And the white city behind us washes its threshold, the
bed of night.

Translated from the French by Kathleen Weaver

Amrita Pritam
India   (b. 1919)

The Breadwinner

My breadwinner
I have eaten your salt
And I must obey the salt
As my father willed,
I am of his blood
And must obey his blood.

Before I can speak
Your bread speaks.
I am ready to speak
But my words are weighed down
By the weight of bread.

My breadwinner
Working child
Follows working father
And I can refuse
No work.

All other work
My hands can do
And this too.

My breadwinner
I am a doll of flesh
For you to play with,
I am a cup of young blood
For you to drink.
I stand before you
Ready for use

According to your will
I grew
And was ground
And kneaded
And rolled out,
You may bake me
In your oven
And eat me like bread;
I am only a scrap of bread
And you are only lava
To cool or grow hot as you will.

As I stand before you
Take me in your arms
Plunge me in the lava of your body
Kiss me
Fondle me
Do with me what you will,
My breadwinner
Do not ask for my love, only make me yours.

Translated from the Punjabi by Charles Brasch with
Amrita Pritam

Sonja Åkesson
Sweden (b. 1926)

The Marital Problem I

Be White Man's Slave.

White Man be nice sometimes, oh yeah,
vacuumclean floors and play cards
with children on Holiday.

White Man be in fucking bad mood
and swear bad words
many days.

White Man not accept sloppy work.
White Man not accept fried Meat.
White Man not accept stupid talk.
White Man have big fit
stumble childrens' boots.

Be White Man's slave.

Bear Another Man's children.
Bear White Man's children.
White Man take care
pay for all the children
Never be free Great Debt
to White Man.

White Man make money at his Works
White Man buy things
White Man buy wife.

Wife wash sauce
Wife cook dirt

Wife do dregs
Be White Man's slave.

White Man think many thoughts, become crazy?
Be White Man's slave.
White Man get drunk break things?
Be White Man's slave.

White Man become tired old breast old stomach
White Man tired old lady
ask go to Hell?
White Man become tired Other Man's children?

Be White Man's slave
Come crawling knees
begging
be White Man's slave.

Translated from the Swedish by Joanna Bankier

Tove Ditlevsen
Denmark   (b. 1918)

Divorce   1

He would
in the case of a divorce
demand half
of everything
he said.
Half a sofa
half a television
half a summerhouse
half a pound of butter
half a child.

The apartment was his
he said
because it was in his name.
The point was
that he loved her.

She loved someone
whose wife would
demand half
of everything.

That was in the marriage law.
It was as clear
as two and two are four.

The lawyer said
that it was right.

She smashed up half
of everything

and tore the tax sheet in pieces.
Then she went out
to the home for women on Jagtvej
with half a child.

The child was teased at school
because he only had
one ear.
Otherwise life could be
put up with in that way
since it could not be
otherwise.

Divorce 3

It is not easy
to be alone
other people
have impatient
waiting-room eyes.
The floor pulls
your steps away
underneath you.
You move
hand over hand
from hour to hour
A vocabulary
of around
a hundred words
was not included
in the division of the household.

The craving for something annoying
the lack of strong smells.
Cold smoke in the curtains.

The bed is
too wide now.
Girlfriends leave
at potato-boiling time.

Freedom
comes first
with the next train
an unknown
traveler
who doesn't
like children.
The dog is
uneasy
sniffs at
the wrong pants legs
is soon
in heat.

You read
books
watch television
take in
nothing
are suddenly
very happy
in the morning
and in despair
before evening.

It's a transition
girlfriends say
something you have
to go through.
Weightless as an
astronaut
you float around
in empty rooms
and wait
for the freedom
to do
what you
no longer
want to do.

Translated from the Danish by Ann Freeman

Marina Tsvetayeva
Soviet Union   (*1894–1941*)

from Epitaph

1

The blow   muffled through years of
    forgetting, of not knowing:
That blow reaches me now like the song of a
    woman, or like horses neighing.

Through an inert building, a song of passion and
    the blow comes:
dulled by forgetfulness, by not knowing, which is
    a soundless thicket.

It is the sin of memory, which has no eyes or
    lips or flesh or nose,
the silt of all the days and nights
    we have been without each other

the blow is muffled with moss and waterweed:
    so ivy devours the
core of the living thing it is ruining
    —a knife through a feather bed.

Window wadding, our ears are plugged with it
    and with that other wool
outside windows of snow and the weight of spiritless
    years: and the blow is muffled.

Translated from the Russian by Elaine Feinstein

Mririda n'Ait Attik
Morocco (*fl. 1940–1945*)

Sister

Sister, don't scold me.
I know I shouldn't have slept in the *azib*.
You know, sister, what can happen there
On a warm night, close to a young man . . .
Am I the only girl to give in
To the wishes of a young man?
How could I know that this night
Would bring a heavy stomach?
Sister, keep my secret!
Old Tamoucha knows the virtues of plants,
Of plants that will quickly deliver me.
Sister, you know well that afterwards
There won't be a trace.
Tamoucha has the alum and resin ready
To restore my virginity.
She has even promised to mention marriage
(Is it possible?) to our dear cousin . . .
Tell me, sister, will he make a good husband?

The Second Wife

She has come, the stranger.
She has taken her place in the house
With her tattoos which are unlike ours.
She is young and beautiful
As my husband wanted.
For their games the nights aren't long enough!

But we'll see if she's as interested in work!
The colors of the clothes and scarves she wears
Are brighter than the colors of the peacock,
But she'll have to get used to coarse wool
And going into the woods
And milking the cows
And cooking . . .
From mouth to ear people blame my husband—
Not for taking a second wife
But for bringing an intruder to the village,
A stranger, of whom nothing is known,
Or very little.
They say she is an Ait Tambout.
Could she not be an Ait Takbout?
Since she came the house has not been the same.
It's as though the walls and floors were sulking.
Perhaps I am the only one who feels it.
My husband is happy with his new wife.

I too was beautiful, but my time has passed.

The Abandoned

Let me weep. He has left.

Why torment yourself like a little girl?
Many go to the forest of Mesgounane,
And a month passes quickly.

My eyes flutter. My heart is clenched.

Why torture yourself for nothing?
Others have gone to the Dra
To fetch dates and henna.

I'll weep till my tears give out.

Why all this sadness for a brief absence?
He will return from the market at Demnat
With his mules packed and a gift for you.

Grief comes over me like rust upon iron.

What is all this? Jealousy?
Give him time to get to Marrakech,
To sell his walnuts and walnut tree bark.

Separation is more bitter than death.

Don't worry this way.
Even if the caid puts him in jail
He will be in your arms before the new moon.

Alas, he is not in the forest.
Nor in the Dra, nor at the market,
Nor in prison. He has left me
To join the army . . . He said,
"Life is too hard in the mountains."
And mine now will be worse than that.

Translated from the Berber into French by René Euloge
English version by Daniel Halpern and Paula Paley

Violeta Parra
Chile *(1917–1967)*

Goddamn the Empty Sky

Goddamn the empty sky
and the stars at night
goddamn the ripply bright
stream as it goes by
goddamn the way stones lie
on dirt or on the street
goddamn the oven's heat
because my heart is raw
goddamn the laws
of time the way they cheat
my pain's as bad as that.

Goddamn the mountain chain
the Andes and the Coast
goddamn Mister the most
and least amount of rain
also crazy and sane
and candor and deceit
goddamn what smells so sweet
because my luck is out
goddamn the lack of doubt
what's messy and what's neat
my pain's as bad as that.

Goddamn the Spring
with its plants in blossom
and the color of Autumn
goddamn the whole damn thing
birds on the wing
goddamn them more and more

'cause I'm really done for
goddamn Winter to bits
along with Summer's tricks
goddamn the saint and whore
my pain's as bad as that.

Goddamn getting on your feet
for the stars and stripes
goddamn symbols of all types
Venus and Main Street
and the canary's tweet
the planets and their motions
the earth with its erosions
because my soul is sore
goddamn the ports and shores
of the enormous oceans
my pain's as bad as that.

Goddamn the moon and weather
desert and river bed
goddamnit for the dead
and the living together
the bird with all its feathers
is such a goddamn mess
schools, places to confess
I tell you what I'm sick of
goddamn that one word love
with all its nastiness
my pain's as bad as that.

So goddamn the number eight
eleven nine and four
choir boys and monsignors

preachers and men of state
goddamn them it's too late
free man and prisoner
soft voice and quarreler
I damn them every week
in Spanish and in Greek
thanks to a two-timer
my pain's as bad as that.

Translated from the Spanish by John Felstiner

Meditations

Sophia de Mello Breyner Andresen
Portugal (*b. 1919*)

Listen

Listen:
Everything is calm and smooth and sleeping.
The walls apparent, the floor reflecting,
And painted on the glass of the window,
The sky, green emptiness, two trees.
Close your eyes and rest no less profoundly
Than any other thing which never flowered.

Don't touch anything, don't look, don't recollect.
One step enough
To shatter the furniture baked
By endless, unused days of sunlight.

Don't remember, don't anticipate.
You do not share the nature of a fruit:
Nothing here that time or sun will ripen.

Translated from the Portuguese by Ruth Fainlight

Marguerite Clerbout
France

Spring in the Woods

Hear one voice
for another
the bird
I do not see
in the branches, from
branch to branch
until silence
comes to the birds
like night to stars

———————

a veil where
winds fall silent
accord
with the bird that
lifts over trees for
silence in song

———————

to wake in a
clouded garden is a dream
only

magnificent fruit

Matinal

a large tree shakes and the
skies move
all
the skies of water

a petal
where the sun
already shines

the light
slips by, the
beautiful shadows last

on the rouge
of leaves
dawn will come

Translated from the French by Kathleen Weaver

Bella Akhmadulina
Soviet Union (*b. 1937*)

Autumn

Not working, not breathing,
the beehive sweetens and dies.
The autumn deepens, the soul
ripens and grows round;

drawn into the turning color of fruit,
cast out of the idle blossoms.
Work is long and dull in autumn,
the word is heavy.

More and more heavily, day by day,
nature weighs down the mind.
A laziness like wisdom
overshadows the mouth with silence.

Even a child, riding along,
cycling into white shafts of light,
suddenly will look up
with a pale, clear sadness.

Translated from the Russian by Barbara Einzig

Silence

Who was it that took away my voice?
The black wound he left in my throat
Can't even cry.

March is at work under the snow
And the birds of my throat are dead,
Their gardens turning into dictionaries.

I beg my lips to sing.
I beg the lips of the snowfall,
Of the cliff and the bush to sing.

Between my lips, the round shape
Of the air in my mouth.
Because I can say nothing,

I'll try anything
For the trees in the snow.
I breathe. I swing my arms. I lie.

From this sudden silence,
Like death, that loved
The names of all words,
You raise me now in song.

Translated from the Russian by Daniel Halpern

Malka Heifetz Tussman
United States (Yiddish) (*b. 1896*)

Water Without Sound

The sea
tore a rib from its side
and said:
Go! lie down there, be
a sign that I
am great and mighty.
Go
be a sign.

The canal
lies at my window,
speechless.

What can be sadder
than water
without sound?

Leaves

Leaves don't fall. They descend.
Longing for earth, they come winging.
In their time, they'll come again,
For leaves don't fall. They descend.
On the branches, they will be again
Green and fragrant, cradle-swinging,
For leaves don't fall. They descend.
Longing for earth, they come winging.

Spoil

The white winter light
hastens the day through the panes,
waking an awareness
that lies dormant
like a bear in winter-sleep.

It slashes into the eye
but rings out no awakened joy.

Such a strict cleanness.

Make a little spot.
Break the white expanse.
Spoil the form purposely,
deliberately.

Then it may
happen—
a poem.

Translated from the Yiddish by Marcia Falk

Natalya Gorbanevskaya
Soviet Union (b. *1936*)

The cricket sings on Twelfth-night,
on a January Monday,
and the ringing of the bells
floats among the snow-drifts,
barely, barely touching
their edges with its wing.

On Twelfth-night sings the cricket,
my chance visitor is silent,
and the ringing of the bells
drowns in the deep snow,
melts in the high sky,
in space that is cornerless.

But, in the corner by the stove,
like homunculi, the crickets
chirp, while all around
the ringing melts, and drowns,
but touches, in departing,
brushes us with its wing.

Translated from the Russian by Daniel Weissbort

Leah Goldberg
Israel   (1911–1970)

Last Brightness

The gleaming of gold deceives—
This is the last brightness.
A glassy blue now crowns
The heads of the mountains.

Another few days, before long,
Stripped trees will be standing
Like ancient, mute instruments
Beautifully strung.

A pale and trembling morning
Will touch chill stone.
And a bird on its way to exile will call
From cold heavens.

Illuminations   2

Across one of the hills
Flies an orange bird
Whose name I do not know.
But the olive trees know her,
The wind, pursuing her, sings:
Your home is here.

In the eyes of a small Arab girl
At the edge of the village in ruins
An orange bird flutters
Whose name I do not know.

Translated from the Hebrew by Robert Alter

Ada Negri
Italy (1870–1945)

Tonight

You who accept the voices of the stars
and of the mud, my God, tonight listen
to the raucous cry of the frogs in the depths
of the gardens, down there in the mud
surge up from the earth's center, earth
of mid May, lovesick earth.
And I am only a little bit of this earth
without beauty, and I do no wrong
if I entreat you with the cry of the frogs
hidden in soft mud at the ditches' edge
humble, yes, but so vast that the shadows
are soaked with it and the clods swell with it
towards the purity of your silences
as the sea does when the moon is full.

Translated from the Italian by Brenda Webster

Teresa Torres
Argentina

Poem

What is hidden in the fruit of summer?
Everything is dying in the flames
of early morning.

A moment of shadows
has settled in the serving dish on the table,
until even the bread is bitter.

Translated from the Spanish by James Tipton

Majken Johansson
Sweden (*b. 1930*)

Proportion Poetry

I wash my hands several times a day
open and close windows
brush my teeth comb and recomb my hair
think food check my stockingseams dust the bookshelf
diligently compose compendiums

days on end

I plant my life in neat seconds
pay close attention to the regular flow of subsidies
secure my social flank

days on end

once by chance once a month
out of the deskdrawer
a half-written poem flies
flaps around the room and
lands on the typewriter

I

wash my hands close the window comb my hair
think
one unplanted untended second without limits
finish off
the poem.

The flank is shaky the flow of subsidies stops
the stockingseam spirals and the bookcase goes crazy

I hold my breath
poem in hand.

and then I breathe
days on end.

Translated from the Swedish by Joanna Bankier

Ellen Warmond

Netherlands (*b. 1930*)

Change of Scene

As soon as the day is shoved
Like blackmail under my door,
The red seals of dreams are cut
By swift sunlit knives.

Wearily houses open their bitter eyes,
And stars fall pallid from their course.

When the silent sentinels
Nightdream and daydream
Hastily trade places,
The firing squad of the twelve
New hours quietly takes aim.

Translated from the Dutch by Manfred Wolf

Nadia Tuéni
Lebanon (*b. 1935*)

Of course
the sun is angry
the moon has slid under the earth
so the wind is a rich man's hand.
Of course
the universe is a simple mirror
and your eyes a feast day.
Of course
death is a misunderstanding
speech an obedient horse.
Of course
the star is a cow's eye
the sky a palace in ruins
Of course
love is a lost bird.

Translated from the French by Carol Cosman

Ingrid Jonker
South Africa (*1933–1965*)

Dark Stream

Green stream full of life
that the sun looks into
with you I cannot talk
you have too many secrets.
Shall I talk with the little tadpoles?
They are too shy.
They say they're going to become big frogs?
It's too uncertain.
Go weep because one sinks
before his back-legs are out?
It's too insignificant.
Stream in which the darkness
sees only the darkness
with you I can speak
I know you better.

*Translated from the Afrikaans by Jake Cope
and William Plomer*

Anne Hébert
Canada (*b. 1916*)

Night

Night
The silence of night
Washes round me
Like great deep sea currents.

I lie in the depths of silent sea-green waters.
I hear my heart
It flares and is extinguished
Like a beacon.

Clouded rhythm
Secret code
I decipher no mystery.

With each burst of light I
Close my eyes
For the flow of evening
Sinking
Through endless silence.

Landscape

Wrapped in anger
Like a filthy coat
I sleep under a rotted bridge
Verdigris, soft lilacs.

Dried sorrows
Algae, o my beautiful dead
Love ground to salt
Hands that are forever lost.

My childhood lifts in smoke from the two banks
Sand, marsh—faint memory
Haunted by the hoarse cry
Of imaginary birds lashed by wind.

Translated from the French by Kathleen Weaver

Eeva-Liisa Manner
Finland (b. 1921)

The skin like burnt glass or
prepared leather
that kind of translucent parchment
which cracks easily and is sewn together
and big running characters
    like eyes
made with so much patience
with a brush thin like a hair
    like the words in the cells at the Dead Sea
I could not read anything
It was Hebrew
I touched the frail seam
the book curled up and gave way
like the leaf of an ashtree in the flame.

––––––––

Do not think I give any importance
to this or any other attempt to surmount the conflict.
The whole intelligence of a poem is in futility:
birds like holes in black snow
on the heart of a cold and long day.

––––––––

Noon goes over the withered earth.
The first hour falls on the page of my book.
It is quiet in the room, the light leaves the window.
Memories come and go
like the wind goes through the forest,
like the wind goes through the forest.

––––––––

The tree has crashed down in the backyard.
The fallen leaves are heaped on the threshold.

I forget where I am,
Voices I can not understand rise to my eyes.

Dark leaves, quiet hours.
Shadows walk on the water, disappear.
The moon is smoky, sleep builds stepping stones.
We go down.

———

Some wine. A bed. Separation from the sounds of the day.
    A curtain.
Night. The Auriga moves to the western edge of the
    window.
The gate of sleep is open, and still the quiet
herds of the animals are gathering under the oaks.

Translated from the Finnish by Jaakko A. Ahokas

Antonia Pozzi
Italy *(1912–1938)*

Awakening

Risen from who knows what shadows
with effort recovering the sense
of your weight
of your warmth
and the night has nothing
for your trouble
but this mad burst
of black rain
and the shriek of wind at the windows.

Where was God?

Translated from the Italian by Brenda Webster

Veronica Porumbacu
Romania (*b. 1921*)

With a Ring

Someone
clinks
a ring of keys
relentlessly
his hand
cuts
a mark
each time I leave
until
one day
a key
turns in the lock
and I can't come back.

Translated from the Romanian by Veronica Porumbacu
and Kathleen Weaver

Isabelle Vuckovic
France

Maturity

We have reached the age
of light meals . . .
the age when a warm bath
lasts the whole morning,
when a taste of wine
justifies life and death—
when, for hours, the mind
toys with twelve syllables
and the broken jasmine flower
satisfies night's desires.

Dahlia Ravikovitch
Israel (b. 1936)

Pride

Even rocks crack, I tell you,
and not because of age.
For years they lie on their backs
in the heat and the cold,
so many years,
it almost seems peaceful.
They don't move, so the cracks stay hidden.
A kind of pride.
Years pass over them, waiting.
Whoever is going to shatter them
hasn't come yet.
And so the moss flourishes, the seaweed swirls,
the sea pushes through and rolls back,
and it seems they are motionless.
Till a little seal comes to rub against the rocks,
comes and goes away.
And suddenly the stone is split.
I told you, when rocks crack it happens by surprise.
And people, too.

Translated from the Hebrew by Chana Bloch

Antonia Pozzi
Italy *(1912–1938)*

Canzonetta

Everyone buys his own
unhappiness
where he wishes—

even in a dark shop
austere
among dusty books
liquidated at half price—

useless books—
all the Greek Tragedies—
but if you don't know Greek
anymore—
can you tell me why you
have bought them?

useless books—
Poetry For Children
with colored soldiers—
but if you don't have
children
yourself
can you tell me why
you have bought them?
if you will never have children
anymore

can you tell me for whom
you have
wasted

your money
this way?

everyone buys his own unhappiness
where he wishes
as he wishes
even
here.

Translated from the Italian by Brenda Webster

Yosano Akiko
Japan *(1878–1942)*

from Tangled Hair: Selected *Tanka*

In my bath—
Submerged like some graceful lily
At the bottom of a spring,
How beautiful
This body of twenty summers.

———

Tears in your eyes
You ask for sympathy;
I look at the waning moon
Reflected
On the lonely lake.

———

Restless night,
My tangled hair
Sounds against my koto!
Is it three months of spring
And not one note struck?

———

Ask me not
If now I write poems—
I am like
Twenty-five koto strings
Without a bridge for sound.

———

Through these pines
The breeze equally
On her cheeks and mine,
Yet how like strangers
Our thoughts.

———

How can I entertain you,
Traveler,
With a story of love?
This courtesan's dreams are threadbare,
Drab, drab green.

———

I pitied him
Standing by the door
In the evening
Calling the name of my sister
Who died last year.

———

Twenty, jealous,
Wilting this summer
In the village heat,
I listen to my husband
Taunt me with Kyoto pleasures!

———

Behind the temple
Where the white bell-flowers bloom,
Who is it
Lamenting the solitude
Of her chosen way?

*Translated from the Japanese by Sanford Goldstein
and Seishi Shinoda*

Hsiung-hung
Taiwan (*b. 1940*)

Written in the Sunset

Time is engraved on the pale green faces
Of the floating lotus leaves.
Our hearts are a sea, a lake,
Finally a little pond, where
Spider webs interlock over the round leaves,
And below them our longing
Is only a single drop of dew.

Sometimes, suddenly the old story overcomes us.
Time triumphs then.
And lets down its hair—
Shadowy black,
Trailing like a willow.

The old melancholy
Comes from the land of longing.
The colors of the sunset thicken.
The shadows grow fast on the water.
You can tear them,
But not tear them away.

*Translated from the Chinese by Kenneth Rexroth
and Ling Chung*

Ping-hsin
People's Republic of China (*b. 1902*)

from Multitudinous Stars and Spring Waters

1
Sprays of frost flowers form
When the North wind blows gently.
2
Void only—
Take away your veil of stars
Let me worship
The splendor of your face.
3
These fragmented verses
Are only drops of spray
On the sea of knowledge.
Yet they are bright shining
Multitudinous stars, inlaid
On the skies of the heart.
4
The orphan boat of my heart
Crosses the unsteady, undulant,
Ocean of Time.
The commonplace puddle
Reflects the setting sun
And becomes the Sea of Gold.
5
Oh little island,
How can you be so secure,
When countless great mountains
Have sunk in the sea?
6
The rose of Heaven—
Its red appears
In contemplative vision.

7
The pine branch of Heaven—
Its green appears
In contemplative vision.
But the Word of Heaven
Is neither written nor read
In contemplative vision.
8
Bright moon—
All grief, sorrow, loneliness completed—
Fields of silver light—
Who, on the other side of the brook
Blows a surging flute?
9
A trellis of sticks
Crowned with chrysanthemums—
Right there,
You can realize all
The self-sufficient universe.

*Translated from the Chinese by Kenneth Rexroth
and Ling Chung*

Anonymous
Trobriand Islands

Song of a Girl Journeying
to the Country of the Dead

Place changes, dawn breaks
Birds are waking.

My chest is marked
handsome boys look away.

Spirit canoe with youngsters
but road leads me away.

Wind whispers, dark cloud meets me
current drags me on.

Translated from the Kiriwina by a native translator,
anonymous

Speaking
for
Others

Anna Akhmatova
Soviet Union   *(1889–1966)*

from Requiem 1935–1940

No, not under an alien sky
not under the protection of alien wings
I lived through that time with my people
where, unhappily, my people were

1
They came for you at daybreak
I walked behind you, as to a funeral
In the dark room the children wept
in the shrine the candle glittered
on your lips the cold of icons
and the deathly sweat on your forehead
I can't forget
I will stand, as the women of the Strel'tsy,
under the Kremlin towers

3
No, it is not I, it is someone else who suffers
it is as though I can not
On whatever it was that happened
let a dark cloth be drawn
let the lights go out . . .
                                        night

4
Was it shown to you, scoffing child,
loved by all your friends,

joyful mischief-maker in the Czar's garden—
what would happen in your life—
that you would stand under the prison wall
with hundreds of others, bundle in arm,
and your hot tears would melt
the ice of a New Year's day
how the prison poplars sway,
and not a sound—but how many
innocent lives ended

6
The weeks fly lightly
I don't understand what happened
how on you, my son, in prison
white nights look down
a hawk eye hot
on your high cross
and they speak of death

7
   Sentence

And the word falls like a stone
on my still living heart
no matter, perhaps I was ready
I will handle this somehow
today I have much to do
must fight each trace of memory
must, so the soul turned to stone
will learn to live again
but not this—hot rustling summer

a celebration outside my window
I long ago had a presentiment—
a day of light and an empty house

Summer 1939

9
Now the wings of madness
                hover in my soul
they hand me wine fire
                and let me float in darkness
and I understand
                that they have the victory
I listen to my own
                as to another's delirium
they don't allow me
                to carry anything
        not a son's terrified eyes
        nor stony suffering
        nor the day of terror
        nor the hour of meeting
        the dear cool hand
        nor the lime tree shaking in shadows
        nor the distant sound
        a last, comforting word

May 4, 1940

Epilogue

and if they close my garrulous throat
crying for millions of others

let them remember me
on the eve of my burial day
but if sometime in this nation
they plan to erect a statue to me
I give permission to celebrate
on this condition: that they place it
not by the sea, where I was born
sea bonds were broken long ago
not on school grounds by the cherished stump
where shadows seek me, inconsolable,
but here, where I stood for three hundred hours
here, where no gates opened for me
or else, in blissful death, I may forget
        the rumbling Black Maria
        the hated banging door
        the howl of an old woman, wounded beast
and let melting snow run down tears
from stone eyelids
let the doves of the prison fly above
and boats quietly glide on the Neva

March 1940

Translated from the Russian by Doris Earnshaw

Sarah Kirsch

East Germany (*b. 1935*)

Before the Sun Rises

Before the sun rises my brothers call the spotted dogs in
the yard blow their hands shake dew from their shoes
before the sun is up my brothers are behind the village
have laid nets in the undergrowth bind a bird up tightly it
is blinded it sings right to the end the brothers fill their
pipes lie in the weeds are patient follow the exquisite me-
lodies there are seven hanging in the net now says the
youngest and cuts himself some ham

But when the full moon is behind clouds my brothers walk
in the woods with the dogs hold the branches back for
each other see a cracked enamel pot in the sky they lay
their hands on the hickory tree pluck a blade of grass blow
deer out into the open and hit them as they learned to with
the first shot come groaning through the yard with a load
as stiff as a board on their backs

My brothers have got yellow greatcoats stars soft creased
boots they carry knapsacks there is a picture of our house
packed inside a tin of meat and their bird net they have
the latest guns go abroad they are to shoot when there is a
man in the sights I know my brothers they hold the
branches back for each other and are patient right to the
end

Translated from the German by Gordon and
Gisela Brotherston

Nina Cassian
Romania (*b. 1924*)

A Man

While fighting for his country, he lost an arm
and was suddenly afraid:
'From now on, I shall only be able to do things by halves.
I shall reap half a harvest.
I shall be able to play either the tune
or the accompaniment on the piano,
but never both parts together.
I shall be able to bang with only one fist
on doors, and worst of all
I shall only be able to half hold
my love close to me.
There will be things I cannot do at all,
applaud for example,
at shows where everyone applauds.'

From that moment on, he set himself to do
        everything with twice as much enthusiasm.
And where the arm had been torn away
a wing grew.

Forūgh Farrokhzād
Iran (*1935–1967*)

I feel sorry for the garden

No one cares about the flowers
no one cares about the fish in the pool
no one wants to see
how the garden's dying
its heart swelling in the hot sun
its feeling not its own, cut off, decaying
its mind slowly, slowly growing empty
　　　　　　　　of memories of green

Our yard stand lonely
our yard yawns
waiting for rain from some still nameless cloud
and the pool in our yard is drying up.
Inexperienced little stars
tumble down from the tops of the trees
and at night comes a sound of coughing
from the pallid windows where the goldfish live.
Our yard stands lonely.

Father says, "My day is past,
my day is past—
I've carried my load,
and done what I had to do"
And he sits all day long in his room
reading old chronicles
or the *Epic of the Kings,*
and he says to Mother:
"To hell with the birds and the goldfish—
When I'm gone, what's it to me
if the garden's there

or ceases to be—
All I want's my retirement check"

My mother's whole life is a prayer rug
spread out on the threshold
of the fear of hellfire
She peers behind everything
looking for traces of sin
and thinks it's the curse of some hidden fault
that's blighted the garden
Mother's a born sinner.
She spends her whole day praying—
she breathes a prayer over all the flowers
and over the goldfish
and over herself
Mother's waiting for the Second Coming
and the blessing from above

My brother calls the garden a graveyard
He laughs at the way the weeds have taken over
and simply numbers
the goldfish corpses
under the scabrous skin of the water
as they change themselves to floating specks of rot
My brother's addicted to philosophy.
He sees the garden's only cure
in its total destruction.
He gets drunk
and bangs on doors and walls
and tries to say
that he's wretched and weary and wracked with despair
He even carries his despair with him
into the streets and bazaars

along with his i.d. and date book and handkerchief and
    lighter and pen
And this despair
is so little
that it loses itself at night in the barroom crowds.

My sister, who used to be friends with the flowers,
and when Mother had spanked her
would take her childish complaint
to their silent, sympathetic council,
and from time to time invited the goldfish
to cookies and sunshine—
now she lives on the other side of town,
with her plastic house
and her plastic fish
and the safe plastic love of her husband,
and in the shade of her plastic trees
she sings plastic songs
and bears real children
Whenever
she comes to see us
and her skirt brushes against the poverty of the garden
she bathes herself in eau de cologne
Whenever
she comes to see us
she's expecting

Our yard stands lonely
Our yard stands lonely
All day
from beyond the gate
come sounds of things exploding and crumbling
Our neighbors are all planting their gardens

with machine guns and mortars
in place of flowers
They are roofing over their tiled pools,
and the pools, without intending,
have turned into secret ammunition dumps
The children on our block
fill their school bags
with homemade bombs
Our yard is dizzy

I'm frightened
of a time that's lost its soul
I'm frightened
at the thought of all these futile hands
at the sight of strangeness in all these faces
I'm as much alone
as a schoolgirl crazy about geometry
I think maybe the garden could be saved
I think
I think
I think . . .
And the garden's heart is swelling in the hot sun
while   slowly   slowly   the garden's mind
grows empty
                    of memories of green

        Translated from the Persian by Deirdre Lashgari

Cheng Min
People's Republic of China   *(1924?)*

The Drought

Hot wind sweeps over the vegetable patches
"Death, death . . ." a whisper everywhere.
A farmer passes by, on his shoulder
A beautiful new water wheel.
Ah, but it's only an infant
That cannot be born.
All the creeks and ditches are bare
Bare to their dry, cracked, mud beds.
Like the white bones of sailors lying
On the bottom of a dried sea
The barren branches stick out on trees.
A calf stands forlorn on the edge of a pond
Gazing at the people, inquiringly.
The creek passes under an arch of interwoven branches,
Passes under a low bridge, and wears the look
Of an old man living in sweet reminiscence,
But brings no sound of rippling laughter.
It passes, like a rude transient carrying no gifts.
All in the field is quiet as death.
On the abandoned land, men
Have nothing more to say to each other.
All sounds, all hopes
Have been entrusted to Heaven where
Only ceaseless hot winds race on treetops
Like so many fleeing feet.
In the hearts of men there is the fear
Of a mother, and her pain
When she hears the silent weeping of the land.

Translated from the Chinese by Kai-yu Hsu

Noémia da Sousa
Mozambique (*b. 1927*)

Our Voice

Our voice lifts
over the white selfishness of men
it is conscious, savage
it lifts over criminal cold
our voice, drenched with the
dew of the bush.

Our blazing voice, sun of Malangas
our voice of drum-beats calling
our voice blade of Maguiguana
our voice, brother, is wakened
cyclone of recognitions.

It lights yellow hyena eyes with guilt
it burns with the gleam of hope
in the dark souls of the desperate
our voice, brother, our voice, a
summoning drum beat.

Our voice
full moon in the night of despair
beacon in the night of tempests
filing through hundred-year-old bars
brother, our voice is a
thousand voices, a
thousand cries of alarm.

Our voice fattened on misery
our voice loosening chains
our black voice Africa
our black voice that cries, cries, cries.

Our voice
that found in the stinking ditch
grief large as the world
of a simple word: Slavery.

Our voice, crying out endlessly
opening paths
our voice *shipalapala*
our voice of drum-beats summoning
our voice, brother,
is a thousand voices that cry
                    cry
                and cry!

Translated from the Portuguese by Jean Todrani and André Joucla-Ruau. English version by Kathleen Weaver.

Alda do Espírito Santo
São Tomé e Príncipe (b. 1926)

Far from the Beach

Dark sea-shelter
of our land, come
kiss the tiny, savage feet
of my parched beaches

Dark bay, sing
the swollen
bellies of my childhood
the fierce
dreams of my small world
cast on the sands
of the brown coast of Gambia
crying on the sands
of the coast of Gambia.

Sing, my child
your howling dream
on the far sands
of the coast of Gambia

Sing your palm roof
at water's edge, your nest
empty on market day

my child,
sing your mother
in the struggle of life
a basket of fish
balanced on her head
in her daily tasks

an infant
on her weaving spine

        and you
my dream
on brown sands
blouse torn in the common fate,
the long wait, thighs
swollen

Mother
walking under the weight of life
walking to sell her fish
        and you
in a boat
bruising dark sea-waters
           oh, the full
net of evening
cascading into my bay
calm mother
        and this fish for sale

Translated from the Portuguese by Kathleen Weaver

Fadwa Tuqān
Palestinian   (*b. 1917*)

from Behind Bars   I

My mother's phantom hovers here
her forehead shines before my eyes
like the light of stars
She might be thinking of me now,
dreaming
                    (Before my arrest
                    I drew letters in a book
                    new and old
                    I painted roses
                    grown with blood
                    and my mother was near me
                    blessing my painting)
I see her
on her face silence and loneliness now
and in the house
silence and loneliness
My satchel there on the bookshelf
and my school uniform
on the hanger
I see her hand reaching out
brushing the dust from it
I follow my mother's steps
and listen to her thoughts
yearn to her arms and the face of day

Translated from the Arabic by Hatem Hussaini

Caroline N. M. Khaketla

Lesotho   (b. 1918)

The White and the Black

While I'm gone, white mother, kill the fattened oxen
And feed your dear ones well, prime meat and curds
Overspilling so the dogs too lap the juice,
And still enough is left to throw a surplus
To your close kin across the seas.

And you, black mother, hold on firm—
There is a mystery in things to come
And a fierce look lights behind your eyes.
As the world-ball turns around and round
The fleeing partridge finds the forbidden grain.

*Translated from the Southern Sotho by Jack Cope
and Dr. Dan Kunene*

Gabriela Mistral
Chile (*1889–1957*)

Sister

Today I saw a woman plowing a furrow. Her hips are broad, like mine, for love, and she goes about her work bent over the earth.

I caressed her waist; I brought her home with me. She will drink rich milk from my own glass and bask in the shade of my arbors growing pregnant with the pregnancy of love. And if my own breasts be not generous, my son will put his lips to hers, that are rich.

Nāzik al-Malā'ikah
Iraq   (b. 1923)

Elegy for a woman
of no importance

When she died no face turned pale, no lips trembled
doors heard no retelling of her death
no curtains opened to air the room of grief
no eyes followed the coffin to the end of the road—
only, hovering in the memory, a vague form
          passing in the lane

The scrap of news stumbled in the alleyways
its whisper, finding no shelter,
lodged obscurely in an unseen corner.
The moon murmured sadly.

Night, unconcerned, gave way to morning
light came with the milk cart and the call to fasting
with the hungry mewing of a cat of rags and bones
the shrill cries of vendors in the bitter streets
the squabbling of small boys throwing stones
dirty water spilling along the gutters
smells on the wind
which played about the rooftops
playing in deep forgetfulness
playing alone

Translated from the Arabic by Chris Knipp and Mohammad
Sadiq

Lucha Corpi
Mexico   (*b. 1945*)

The Marina Poems

I. *Marina Mother*

They made her of the softest clay
and dried her under the rays of the tropical sun.
With the blood of a tender lamb
her name was written by the elders
on the bark of that tree
as old as they.

Steeped in tradition, mystic
and mute she was sold—
from hand to hand, night to night,
denied and desecrated, waiting for the dawn
and for the owl's song
that would never come;
her womb sacked of its fruit,
her soul thinned to a handful of dust.

You no longer loved her, the elders denied her,
and the child who cried out to her "Mama!"
grew up and called her "whore."

II. *Marina Virgin*

Of her own accord, before the altar
of the crucified god she knelt.
Because she loved you, she only saw
the bleeding man, and loved in him
her secret and mourning memory of you.

She washed away her sins
with holy water, covered her body
with a long, thick cloth
so no one would know
her brown skin had been damned.

Once, you stopped to wonder
where her soul was hidden,
not knowing she had planted it
in the entrails of that earth
her hands had cultivated—
the moist, black earth of your life.

III. *The Devil's Daughter*

When she died, lightning struck in the north,
and on the new stone altar the incense burned
all night long. Her mystic pulsing
silenced, the ancient idol
shattered, her name
devoured by the wind in one deep mutter
(her name so like the salt depths of the sea)—
little remained. Only a half-germinated seed.

IV. *She (Marina Distant)*

She. A flower perhaps, a pool of fresh water . . .
a tropical night,
or a sorrowful child, enclosed

in a prison of the softest clay:
mourning shadow of an ancestral memory,
crossing the bridge at daybreak,
her hands full of earth and sun.

Translated from the Spanish by the author and Catherine
Rodríguez-Nieto

Gabriela Mistral
Chile (1889–1957)

Stranger

"She speaks in a slight accent about her wild seas
with God knows what seaweeds and God knows what
    sands;
so old it's as if she herself were dying,
she prays to a god with no volume and no weight.
She has sown cactus and claw-like grasses
in gardens of ours that she makes strange.
She draws her breath from the panting of the desert
and loves with a passion all that it whitens,
all that never says anything and if it should
it would be like the map of another planet.
Were she to live in our midst for eighty years
it would be always as though she had just come,
speaking in a language that pants and moans
and that is understood only by beasts.
And some night when her suffering is greatest
from a death both silent and strange,
she is going to die right here among us
with nothing but her fate for a pillow."

Translated from the Spanish by Langston Hughes

Saniya Sālih
Syria

Exile

For grief
he wore those colorful bells,
a mask of joy.
He bound his stories
        to his tongue's tip
so they would not betray him
        at the crucial moment.
And he walked
    lightly
        in jewel-studded shoes—
alone as the night
with no stars waiting
but my eyes.

Bird, hovering over the horizon
remember
bullets are everywhere—
Remember
me
    the perpetual traveler—
        All my life
I have willed to go forward and have not
advanced beyond
the borders of my grave.

Translated from the Arabic by Kamal Boulatta

Etel Adnan
Lebanon (*b. 1925*)

The Enemy's Testament

I
With no other identity than the
        letters of V.C.
which sound like venereal disease:

I have been softened up,
my backbone as soft as my belly,

I have been gassed,
my eyes as blind as a worm's,

I have been brainwashed,
told of freedom until light
        passed out of my brain,

I have been shot,
more bullet holes in my flesh
        than holes in a target.

2
They got me out of my lair
for I was infesting my own land,
and they, the foreigners, came to
liberate me,
        liberate me of my share.

3
So now I have this will to make:

I send my brain to your center of research
so they could see what made me fight,
I send my eyes to your President
so they can look him in the face,

       they only knew the darkness of tunnels . . .

I send my teeth to your generals,
they bit more rifle than bread,

       for hunger was my companion . . .

I send my tongue to your cardinals,
it will tell them what Jesus said,

       about the sword . . .

My body, I leave to the Mekong River.

                      Translated by the author

Hien Luong
Vietnam (mid–twentieth century)

Songs That Cannot Be Silenced

Sing! Let us sing out,
Sing out again so our hearts may burst into flame
And our burning blood may finally melt these chains.
So that in the depth of the blackest night
The sun shines forever.

Here they come with their sticks
In the glacial silence
In the bolted cell
Their bloodshot eyes rivet on us
They hurl threatening words,
"Who's the bitch who had the nerve to sing?"

Mute rage engulfs our hearts
Our retort:
A willful silence.

After vain threats and questionings
Blows rain down.
So much flesh is torn
Over all the body, so much pain!

Then, my sister,
You stood up proud
Rising above the pack of killers
"Down with terror! Down with the brutes!"

Hand in hand,
Shoulder to shoulder:
A human wall

Will not give way.
Scarcely have they turned on their heels
Our laughter bursts out more brightly
Our voices rise more sweetly
More harmonious together
With a stronger beat
Defying the impotent rage of the guards.

Such power in such frail bodies—
Does it come from magic?

The next day, reprisals.
Aged mothers,
Little sisters, barely thirteen years old,
Beaten with the rest
Just for having sung.
"Who led the singing?"

Answer: a willful silence.
Cornered between the wall and the hard ground
They fell unconscious.
Awakening,
Into their ears glides the sweet lullaby of an elder sister
Like the voice of the native village.
Suddenly, on your trembling lips
Blooms the rose of a first smile
That no chains nor shackles can imprison!

Translated from the Vietnamese by a native translator,
anonymous

Li Chü
People's Republic of China   (mid-twentieth century)

Harvesting Wheat for
the Public Share

It is a year of good harvest.
The wheat is brought to the threshing yard.
The second sister crushes it.
The elder sister threshes it.
The third sister winnows it
Very carefully and throws away the husks.
The golden grain piles high in the yard.
Round, round wheat, better than pomegranate seeds.
Bite it with your teeth, it goes "go-pou!"
The first pile of wheat is really lovely.
After we have dried it in the sun,
And cleaned it,
We will turn it in as the public share.

*Translated from the Chinese by Kenneth Rexroth and
Ling Chung*

Visions

Natalya Gorbanevskaya
Soviet Union   (b. 1936)

In the bird scream and whistle,
Opening the window, I open myself.
Before the grand presence passing by
I hide, like a farmyard fowl.

The white flame of flight
fades. The transcendental howl
subsides. In the empty sky
a magpie wags its tail.

Translated from the Russian by Daniel Weissbort

Else Lasker-Schüler
Germany   *(1869–1945)*

The Shulamite

O, from your sweet mouth I have come
To know beatitude so well!
Already I feel the lips of Gabriel
Burning on my breast . . .
And the night-clouds drink
My deep dream of cedars.
O, how your life beckons me!
And I vanish
With flowering heartache,
I blow away into space,
Into time,
To forever,
And my soul burns away in the evening colors
of Jerusalem.

Translated from the German by Robert Alter

Simone Weil

France *(1909–1943)*

Illumination

Let the pure sky ahead, this sky of long
and sweeping clouds, send to me
a wind so strong, a wind the scent of joy;
let all be born now, cleansed of dreams.

Human cities will be born for me
blown clean of mist,
the roofs, the cries, the steps, the hundred lights,
the human sounds: what time consumes.

Oceans will be born, the rocking boat,
the oars' dip, the fires of the night,
fields will be born, loose sheaves flung;
evenings will be born, star by star.

The lamp will be born and bended knees,
darkness, shock at the face turned away,
hands will be born, metals pounded hard,
iron bitten in the cry of the machines.

The world is born; wind, let it endure!
But phantoms cover it again, the world
that was born for me among the clouds
in a fissure of pale green sky.

Translated from the French by Carol Cosman

Simone Weil
France   (*1909–1943*)

from Random Thoughts on the Love of God

. . . Creatures speak in sounds. The word of God is silence. The secret word of God's love can be nothing but silence. Christ is the silence of God. There is no tree like the cross. No harmony like the silence of God. The Pythagoreans knew this harmony in the endless silence that surrounds the stars. Necessity, here below, is the resonance of God's silence.

Our soul makes constant noise, but it has a silent place we never hear. When the silence of God enters us, pierces our soul and joins its silent secret place, then God is our treasure and our heart. And space opens before us like a fruit that breaks in two. Then we see the universe from a point beyond space.

Ping-hsin
People's Republic of China (b. 1902)

Receiving Buddha

On the altar
faint stars of fire burning
heads bowed in subdued worship.

'Where do I come from?
where am I going?
is there no return—
no end to this endless ring of dusty life?'

Gone   the shadows of illusion
gone   the sounds of the myriad things
faintly, vaguely rising
out of the canopy of gold, the screen of pearls:
Buddha's image emerging.

To ask
'Where do I come from?
where am I going?'—
this wheeling ring of dusty life—
will close the path of return
for all the multitude.

In this world
the path of arrival is the path of departure
the path of departure will be the path of arrival.

Translated from the Chinese by K. C. Leung

Antonia Pozzi
Italy *(1912–1938)*

Landing

Dull swish of runners
over the buried
lake:

behind us
the narrow track
vanishes in a flurry of snow.

Now the sound rises
of an assault in the pass.

A rhythmic screech:
perhaps the icy weeping of the bivouacs
cry of fearful storms;
or the lament of birds
hoarse pant
of slender foxes seen dying—

Are we not going to a landsend?

And when in other garb
I will pause at the warm windows—
(the sled will have carried me off
in the whirl of its bells,
I will have at my shoulders
lights   faces   songs)

my shadow
will be on the lake
motionless pledge of me
outside—in the cruel
legendary night.

Translated from the Italian by Brenda Webster

Alfonsina Storni
Argentina *(1892–1938)*

Dog and Sea

Alone the sea
and the sky alone;
and all was a grey, chill
space
and I could hear nothing
nor could see
more than that grey,
monotonous
and lifeless.

By my side
the dog, against the wind,
was howling, and his barking
shook the dead waves;
his whine
cut a path
in the lead air;
and his ears, tense,
seemed to rise like antennae
toward dismantled
throats.

Were there nests
of live mice
where my eyes,
dry,
could not reach?

Ghosts, cradling themselves
on the distant

peaks
of sea?

And did subterranean faces
appear in the wall
of wind?

And did someone
garb the sea,
line
its face of shadows
deepest down
with multicolored parks?

This time
an endless howling,
his head erect;
he rose
as if somehow
ordered to leave
and tore away
toward the town
fleeing that sea.

And at this abandoning,
my heart
crazily, without cause,
took flight,
a bell of shadows.

Translated from the Spanish by Mark I. Smith

Veronica Porumbacu
Romania (*b. 1921*)

White Bears

Now
the polar nights
startle the
sleeping trees
the sky itself hurls the
sun-disc: balloon
among white bears. Look—
look how they strip off their fur,
naked they
play with emotions.

*Translated from the Romanian by Veronica Porumbacu
and Kathleen Weaver*

Nelly Sachs
Germany (*1891–1969*)

In the blue distance

In the blue distance
where the red row of apple trees wanders
—rooted feet climbing the sky—
the longing is distilled
for all those who live in the valley.

The sun, lying by the roadside
with magic wands,
commands the travelers to halt.

They stand still
in the glassy nightmare
while the cricket scratches softly
at the invisible

and the stone dancing
changes its dust to music.

But look

But look
but look
man breaks out
in the middle of the market place
can you hear his pulse beating
and the great city
on rubber tires

girded about his body—
for fate
has muffled
the wheel of time—
lifts itself
on the rhythm of his breathing.

Glassy displays
broken raven-eyes
sparkle
the chimneys fly black flags
at the grave of air.

But man
has said *Ah*
and climbs
a straight candle
into the night.

Translated from the German by Ruth and Matthew Mead

Katerina Anghelaki-Rooke
Greece   (*b. 1939*)

Diogenes

By the day I perish in the barrel
I have no imitators in the dark.
Mother's tabernacle has hardened
still I inhabit it
seeing that I was never born
but merely exist
and hurt each time
I touch the walls of the world.
Sprinkled with a few crumbs of light
for hours on end I watch the skin breathe
and more,
and more irascible lines
of my fate,
lines without future in the palm
because I have never hoped
never begun to weave
lies round the nakedness
of my death.
An aged embryo
wrapped in black stuff
daily the cloth unfurled
and it came up to my eyes.
Each day
I twist and turn, groan,
bite my tail
within these 24 hours
I say goodbye, pray for
just so much space and energy,
so much passion
so much, no more

until tomorrow.
This day secured
moves
and changes color, light,
murders me, and I study it
humiliates me and I accept it.
I learn in the space of a span,
at a single ring of age.

There is nothing beyond the barrel,
creaking in the north wind
crackling in the heat
I roll on, roll on
with my celestial space about me
beyond the specific.
No one has ever moved
in the eternity of Nature;
I remember genesis
like last year's fiesta,
about me the sun describes
the orbit of a bug,
always about me
and I the grilled center
live as though I knew
sleep as if I had made answer,
dream in my sleep
of my dead
dying again,
wake and doubt,
sink back into the wooden gut.
Orphaned thus in the gloom,
the counsel of friends is lost me
in the larynx of the night owl

with its untamable wisdom
it cries "transitory"
things always adopt
me transitorily.
Prettily mirrored the world
in the round eye of the cow
as with her four legs
she marks out the meadow definitively,
but I have lost
the magic of appearances
and the depth that draws downward
joins with the seed
beyond death.

Translated from the Greek by Peter Dreyer

Margit Szécsi
Hungary   (b. 1928)

The Death of Moses

I never saw that stone tablet.
I dreamt of it. The lawless existence,
the bared knives, the released bombs,
I lived opposing blighted reality
and dreamt of The Law. And I saw,
I saw in my dream the winding lilies
of Roman numerals. And the Angel's
wing flapped. Then I went down from
the mountain. But merely a 29¢ pen's
silver rocket poises between my fingers.
Just what I can write can be the law.
No godlike thing's above, there isn't
a stone tablet, and no one ever saw it.
We alone are here,
the unplanned chain of sin we emit,
chance as it solidifies to history.
I am the powerless Moses
and you sacrifice to the golden calf.

Translated from the Hungarian by Laura Schiff

Dahlia Ravikovitch
Israel   (*b. 1936*)

How Hong Kong Was Destroyed

I am in Hong Kong.
There's a river here swarming with snakes.
There are Greeks, Chinese, Negroes.
Carnival dragons
gape at the paper lanterns.
Who said they eat you alive here?
A great crowd went down to the river.
You've never seen such silk in your life,
redder than poppy blossoms.

In Hong Kong
the sun rises in the East
and they water the flowers with a perfumed spray
to improve their scent.
But in the evening the paper lanterns
are battered by the wind,
and if someone's murdered, they ask,
Was it a Chinaman? a Negro?
Did he die in pain?
Then they pitch his body into the river
and all the reptiles feed.

I am in Hong Kong.
In the evening the café lights dimmed
and paper lanterns were ripped in the streets.
The land kept erupting and seething
erupting and seething
and I alone knew
that there is nothing in the West
and nothing in the East.

The paper dragon yawned
but the earth erupted.
A horde of enemies will come here
who've never seen silk in their lives.

Only the little prostitutes
still receive their guests
in dresses of soiled silk
in tiny alcoves crowded with lanterns.
Some of them sob when morning comes
over their rotting flesh.
And if someone's killed, they ask,
Oh-oh, Chinese? Negro? Poor thing.
Let's hope he didn't die painfully.
And at dusk the first
of the visitors arrive
like a thorn in the living flesh.

I am in Hong Kong
and Hong Kong hangs on the ocean
like a colored lantern on a hook
at the end of the world.
Perhaps the dragon
will swathe it in crimson silk
and let it drop
into the abyss of the stars.
And only the little prostitutes will sob into the silk
because even now
still now
men pinch them in the belly.

I am not in Hong Kong
and Hong Kong is not in the world.

Where Hong Kong used to be
there's a reddish stain
half in the water and half in the sky.

Translated from the Hebrew by Chana Bloch

Eeva-Liisa Manner

Finland (*b. 1921*)

from Cambrian

A Suite About the Sea and the Animals

VI *Apathy*

The distance from Satan to God
has grown shorter,
the summits are worn out
and the rifts
are full of crumbs.
Smooth. Brown.
Heat only vibrates
and is wrapped around everything
like a burning disgust.
The brain suffers,
not much,
like an oyster perhaps.

We wander along the edge of emptiness.
The legions of the ants
charge and disappear.
The Philistines.
The Holy Scarab rolls
For the greater glory of God.
We see all this
we wander
holding hands
I
and the other.

VII   *And So the Oracles*

We are sailing. Already
we see the Hellespont looming ahead.
The sun spreads on the sea
like a bloody sacrifice.
Magic and smoky
oracles
are honored, a future knowledge.
Temples with many gods
are mumbling prayers.
But the hills, the hips
are dreaming of peace,
not of a fruit.

The shellfish are one with the stone.
The lazy bodies of the crocodiles
nail themselves to the rock
with hot jaws and impatient tails.
The greedy necks
stretch out only after swallows, after music.
Too late.
Limestone is already flowing in the nails.
They are petrified.
And so the oracles.

But when night comes,
Poseidon spurs the monsters
and rides away.
Nothing is dead.
Waves roll in the stone,
a wind and a tempest blow in the atoms.

The harness is loosened, and the movement, and the
    strength.

The nursing bird spreads out her wings
and covers the crawling souls
with their sucking mouths and groping brains.
Worlds are prepared.
Men
the mammals with many vertebrae
are further painfully bred
confused, wondering what is to come.

Translated from the Finnish by Jaakko A. Ahokas

Amy Károlyi
Hungary   (*b. 1909*)

from The Third House

I

Like a cloud hunted by the moon
The two lovely houses of my life scatter:
Fleecy-sky youth
and my years' stifling electric summer—
Look, like grapes in a vat,
I am crowned with grape leaves.

(The steps deceive. They rise up
but end in a valley.
In the depth the old man gnaws an acorn.
His nose dripping
he sprawls on brushwood.

O, where's the sun, the sweet flesh of the bun?
Like a piece of bread the day has gone)

This porch is still cordial,
the sun is broiling,
the stone is still roasting,
the full moon is linen bright,
but the crickets already cry at night,
the fragrance of plums dissolves to alcohol—
O, things, their color-changingness!

Jesus Christ in a wafer sleeps
a wafer-colored stripe darts
under the round lathed sky
his stripe flows in our eyes
the old women's cold slobber

drools on the apron of the year.
Now just the crust is left.
Like a piece of bread the day gives out.

V

Coffee-stained, knife-cut tablecloth
my life sways on the years' clothesline
much washed faded linen
but my death, a gold and diamond jeweled flag,
waving greets me.
This flapping
(a clattering of basalt claws on silver stones)
why does the heart dread it?
Listen your friends are coming for you
from the stove the fire escapes
from the faucet water gently issues
from the ceiling heaven stoops
from your narrow niche you walk into light.

Why does he whom God keeps calling to his honeycomb
whine like a fly glued to flypaper?

VI

Jewel towers relay to jewel towers
the peal of bells
all starting out at noon
they meet, like pious old friends,
in the summer air.

The fine veil from Saint Peter's well
hits, sprays our dusty skin—

(yet holy water doesn't renew the traveller
when his stomach grumbles)

Protectress of travellers
dark Mary in a gold house
pitch-black queen of heaven and earth
glittering in a sacred box
in your slippery gold-leaf mantle
in ice metal and ice brilliance
cover us with your dew-pure eyes.

with prism tears
the travellers pray
in dusty shoes

Jewel towers and umbrella trees of mourning
on the seven hills
bright stockings on the Corso Umberto
budding oleander at the edge of the road
under the sacristies, red crypts

Even in Rome man dies.

Translated from the Hungarian by Laura Schiff

Ágnes Nemes Nagy
Hungary   (b. 1922)

Ikhnaton's Night

Ascending and descending you take shape
Living Sun
In the dark you die, in light you resurrect
You throb in my heart
(Ikhnaton's Hymn to the Sun)

When he went down to the square, the pavilions now
were drenched in the lantern lights,
candles erect in the necks of bottles,
a summer All Saint's Day light,
on plank shelves, in dust,
rose crêpe-paper dolls.

Side of hills tattooed,
hearts stippled on olive-green melon
skins, punctured by knitting needles.
Above, the rippling hair of neon lights.
Hot wind. Scrap of straw.
This night was dark.

He went as if trapped
in the disguise of his shape,
he went motionless. An elevated
train streaked above.

                    "Clean your face.
            Put it in the cave of your palms,
            the will is striated,
            lead it to water like a bird,
            lead it to water like an animal,

wash, wash your face,
every ray of the sun ends in a tiny hand,
with the hands of the sun your face shall be . . ."

Night, its leaden drapes
hang between the lights
between the counters
that gleam like ribbon-candy, like caterpillars,
stifling of candles, rush of wind.

"In the ancient garden
in the garden 100,000 things
under the wafer-colored sky
and you have to swallow the other face
and the green flower, the elder tree
on which Judas hanged himself,
and above the star's bit of green
the unmeasurable in the garden,
if only you could be so minute, my love,
like a god in a wafer."

And now the tanks came.
                                    Hills of metal waves
the streets ran from them in stone basins,
soft bodies ran between metal and stone
each one lugging a balloon bundle,
the clatter of falling canvas stalls,
splash of bridge rails,
ashes in the distance, the fine rain of glass,
and between the intervals, there is that which blares
above them
that which blares
above the entire planet.

And he hurtled himself over the parapet
together with the others,
headlong they rolled together,
jaggedly, jolting they fell
on top of each other,
like a machine-gun burst,
an avalanche.

It was foggy when he began to see again.
He lay on the shore. Reeds.
Another body was beside him in the mud,
stretched on its back, so stiffly
as if private snow had fallen on it.
He got up from it. In a single motion
he rose like smoke,
beside or from the body.
He was so transparent.
He rose and lay in a single motion.

And he took it, even when he departed
Arcanely, he took the body with him.
Between the long ribbons of fog
he went leading himself
                left hand held by his right.

Translated from the Hungarian by Laura Schiff

Notes

"Sonnet to Eurydice" (p. 14). *Eurydice:* Wife of Orpheus, the musician of Greek myth. Soon after their marriage, Eurydice died; determined to rescue her, Orpheus descended to the underworld and was permitted to lead her back to life, provided he did not look at her until the end of their journey. Not hearing her footsteps behind him, he looked back, and she disappeared.

"To Julia de Burgos" (p. 15). *Rocinante:* Don Quixote's broken-down horse, in Cervantes' *Don Quixote.*

"Song for a Young Girl's Puberty Ceremony" (p. 39). The Papago are a desert-dwelling people of the southwest. (The name "Papago" is derived from words meaning "the bean people," a reference to their most important crop.) The Papago songs in this anthology were collected by Frances Densmore in 1920 at San Xavier, near Tucson, Arizona.

The puberty ceremony of the Papago called for a young girl, on her maturity, to be isolated for four days, receiving instruction from an older woman of the tribe. A feast was then given, with four nights of song and dancing. The principal songs, like this one, were received in dreams.

"Song for a Girl on Her First Menstruation" (p. 40). Boikin is one of the more than 650 languages spoken in New Guinea and the adjacent islands.

"Pregnant Woman" (p. 41). *Kukumakrankas:* A Hottentot word for a beautiful starlike flower (*Gethyllis afra*) which dies away and is replaced by a small aromatic fruit pushing up from the sand.

"Song for Bringing a Child into the World" (p. 44). The Seminoles are a Muskhogean tribe originally made up of Creek immigrants to Florida. In 1830 the United States government forcibly relocated the Seminoles to Oklahoma; their numbers were severely reduced in their war to resist this removal. This song was collected by Frances Densmore in 1932 or 1933 in the Big Cypress Swamp region of Florida. The singer was Susie Tiger, a Seminole woman born at the time of the migration to Oklahoma, who sang this song to aid childbirths.

"song of the old woman" (p. 51). This is one of 850 Eskimo poems collected by Paul-Emile Victor at Angmagssalik, on the east coast of Greenland in 1935, and published in French translation in *Poèmes esquimaux* (Paris: Pierre Seghers, 1951).

"This evening" (p. 59). *A Passion crosses the desert, led by a Magus:* The Magi, or Wise Men, visited and paid homage to the Christ child twelve days after his birth. The Passion is Christ's crucifixion.

"Love Charm Songs" (p. 62). The Chippewa are a people of the Upper Great Lakes region, also known as the Ojibwa. The songs here were all collected by Frances Densmore during 1907, 1908, and 1909 on the White Earth, Leech Lake, and Red Lake reservations in northern Minnesota.

"My Love Has Departed" (p. 62). *loon:* An aquatic bird known for its strange cry, which is often compared to laughter.

"Why Should I Be Jealous" (p. 62). According to Chippewa legend, in former times an Indian girl would lie face down on the prairie for hours at a time singing this song.

"I'm Taking Off . . ." (p. 64). *calm as a witch at Easter:* According to a Swedish legend, the forces of evil are let loose every year from Good Friday to Easter Sunday night. The witches are said to fly on broomsticks to Blåkulla, an imaginary mountaintop, where they meet their master, Satan, and perform travesties of Christian ceremonies. *Cambrian:* The first geological period in the Paleozoic Era, marked by the appearance of the first simple marine and animal life.

"I discover you in bits and pieces" (p. 69). *alembic:* An apparatus for distilling, associated with alchemy.

"Love" (p. 70). The poet belongs to the Swedish-speaking community in Finland, which has a long cultural tradition as a result of Swedish political domination that ended in 1809.

"Poem of the End" (p. 77). *for Charon, the price of Lethe:* In Greek mythology, Charon was the ferryman who rowed the spirits of the dead across the rivers of the underworld. The dead were buried with coins under their tongues to pay the fare. Before departure, the spirits drank from the river Lethe (oblivion) to lose all memory of their lives on earth.

"The Breadwinner" (p. 83). *Punjabi:* The language spoken in the northwestern regions of India and Pakistan. It is also the official language of the Punjab state in India.

"Divorce 1" (p. 87). *Jagtvej:* A street in Copenhagen, Denmark.

"Sister" (p. 92). *azib:* A sheepfold.

"The Second Wife" (p. 93). *Ait Tambout/Ait Takbout:* Berber tribes.

"The Abandoned" (p. 93). *Mesgounane:* A forest in Morocco. *the Dra:* Oued Draa, a *wadi* or usually dry riverbed running from the High Atlas Mountains to the Atlantic Ocean near Cape Dra. *Demnat:* An important trading center in westcentral Morocco at the foot of the High Atlas Mountains. *Marrakech:* Chief city of southern Morocco and capital of Marrakech province. *caid:* Berber tribal chief.

"Goddamn the Empty Sky" (p. 95). *monsignors:* Honorific title given to prelates, officers of the Papal court and household, and other clerics.

"The cricket sings on Twelfth-night" (p. 108). *Twelfth-night:* Epiphany, the festival commemorating the visit of the Magi to the Christ child; it is celebrated on January 6, the twelfth day after Christmas. *homunculi:* perfectly-formed though very tiny men.

"The skin like burnt glass or" (p. 119). *in the cells at the Dead Sea:* a reference to the Dead Sea Scrolls, manuscripts and papyri discovered in a cave near the Dead Sea in 1947.

"Some wine. A bed. Separation from the sounds of the day." (p. 120). *The Auriga:* A constellation in the northern sky, also known as The Waggoner.

"Tangled Hair" (p. 127). *tanka:* A five-line, thirty-one-syllable poem, for centuries a major verse form of Japan. *koto:* A thirteen-string plucked instrument tuned by movable bridges; often called a horizontal harp. *Kyoto:* Former capital of Japan, the center of imperial culture.

"Multitudinous Stars and Spring Waters" (p. 130). *rose of Heaven/pine branch of Heaven/Word of Heaven:* Archetypes of the Buddhist cosmic system.

"Song of a Girl Journeying to the Country of the Dead" (p. 132). The *Trobriand Islands* are in the South Pacific, a hundred miles east of New Guinea. *My chest is marked:* The girl is decorated for funeral rites.

"Requiem 1935–1940" (p. 135). *icon:* Religious image painted on wood, venerated in Russian Orthodox homes and churches. *Strel'tsy:* The bodyguard of the Czars. They revolted against Peter the Great in 1698; the revolt was crushed and hundreds were executed. *Neva:* The river running through Leningrad.

"I feel sorry for the garden" (p. 141). *Epic of the Kings:* A poem in 120,000 lines by Firdausi (c. 940–1020) which tells of the lives of the ancient Persian kings.

"Our Voice" (p. 146). *Maguiguana:* Warrior chief during the resistance movement of the Mozambique people against the Portuguese colonialists at the end of the nineteenth century. *shipalapala:* Horn made out of the horn of an antelope.

"Far from the Beach" (p. 148). *Gambia:* A Republic in West Africa.

"The Marina Poems" (p. 154). Doña Marina was a young Indian woman given in slavery to Hernán Cortés after his arrival in Mexico. She served him as guide, interpreter, comrade-at-arms, and nurse throughout the conquest, and bore him a son. When Cortés was preparing his marriage to a Spanish lady of noble rank, he made a gift of land to Marina and married her to one of his lieutenants. Contemporary accounts of the conquest speak of the extraordinary beauty, intelligence, and generosity of this woman, but the attitude of subsequent generations of Mexicans toward her has been ambivalent. She is both idolized as a mother-goddess and reviled as a traitor—her Indian name, Malinche, has become a synonym for treachery.

"The Enemy's Testament" (p. 159). *V.C.:* An abbreviation for Viet Nam cong san, or Viet Cong, a term used by the Western press for adherents of the National Liberation Front, which fought against U.S. forces in Vietnam.

"The Shulamite" (p. 168). *Schulamite:* The name given to the female figure or bride who speaks in the *Song of Songs* or *Song of Solomon,* one of the late books of the Old Testament. According to mystical readings of the text, the Shulamite is Israel giving herself to God, her divine lover.

"Random Thoughts on the Love of God" (p. 170). *Pythagoreans:* In the Pythagorean system, the universe is bounded by a finite crystalline sphere in which are set the "fixed stars" and which rotates about a central fire; the "wandering stars," or planets, are set into inner spheres which also rotate. The vibrations

caused by this motion were called the "music of the spheres."
"Diogenes" (p. 178). *Diogenes:* Cynic philosopher (c. 400 B.C.)
who taught that to free the soul as far as possible, things of the
flesh should be reduced to bare necessities. According to
legend, he lived in a tub and wandered through the streets,
carrying a lantern in the daytime, in search of an honest man.
"Cambrian" (p. 185). *Cambrian:* see note to "I'm Taking Off" p.
196. *The Holy Scarab:* Scarab beetles feed on manure and roll
together balls of dung in which to lay their eggs. In ancient
Egypt, the golden scarab was regarded as sacred. As one of the
forms in which the sun-god appeared, it was a symbol of im-
mortality. *oracle:* The means by which a god speaks, or the
place where the divine will is made known. The most famous
oracle in Classical literature was at Delphi. *Hellespont:* The an-
cient name for the Strait of the Dardanelles connecting the
Aegean and Black Seas. *Poseidon:* In Greek mythology, the
violent, ill-tempered god of the sea.
"The Third House" (p. 188). *Saint Peter's Well:* A fountain in
Rome. *Corso Umberto:* A street in Rome.
"Ikhnaton's Night" (p. 191). *Ikhnaton:* Or Akhenaton, Pharaoh
of Egypt, 1379–1362 B.C. A religious reformer, he replaced
worship of the old Egyptian gods with that of Aton (or Amen),
an obscure sun-deity, creating perhaps the first monotheistic
religion in history. Aton was depicted as the sun-disc, with rays
extending down to earth and ending in hands. *A god in a
wafer:* an allusion to the ceremony of the Eucharist, in which a
wafer of unleavened bread is transsubstantiated into the body
of Christ. *the tanks came:* An allusion to the Second World
War.

Biographies
and Selected Bibliography

The biographies of the poets are brief introductory sketches. Information about several of the poets has proven scarce or unobtainable; we regret this, and hope that readers who know more about a poet will tell us. Oriental names are written with the family name first; for example, Yosano Akiko, Cheng Min, Hien Luong, Li Chu, but not Ping-hsin or Hsiung-hung, which are single pen names. The selected bibliography lists the first published work, if known; the most influential subsequent volumes; collected works; biographies and books of translations in English; and the anthologies where translations may be found. Original titles are given in romanized form, with an English translation. In most cases, the poet's works have not been translated, but interested readers may find translations of individual poems in journals such as *Modern Poetry in Translation* and *Contemporary Literature in Translation*.

Sonja Åkesson (also *Aakesson*) b. Butle, Sweden, 1926. Has published prose, poetry and songs; her volume of poetry *Husfrid* received attention for its introduction into Swedish poetry of a colloquial idiom describing ordinary people in a sterile modern environment. *Situationer* (Situations), 1957; *Husfrid* (Peace in the House), 1963; *Slagdänger* (Streetballads), 1969; *Man får vara glad och tacka Gud* (Collected Poems: We Must Be Content and Thank God), 1967.

Etel Adnan b. Beirut, Lebanon, 1925. Educated in French schools in Lebanon, and in France and the U.S. Professor of French literature and philosophy in the U.S. between 1958 and 1972, when she returned to Beirut. Short-story writer and tapestry designer as well as poet. Has worked as correspondant for *Jeune Afrique* and as cultural editor of Beirut French newspaper *Orient le Jour*. *Moonshots*, 1966; *Five Senses for One Death*, 1973; *Jebu* (in French), 1973; *For Neruda, for Chile*, ed. Lowenfels (translations of some poems), 1975.

Bella Akhmadulina b. Moscow, U.S.S.R., 1937. Educated at the Gorky Institute; has been married to and divorced from the poet Yevgeny Yevtushenko; subsequently married to writer Yuri Nagibin; was admitted to the Writers' Union as a translator rather than as a poet. *Struna* (The String), 1962; *Uroki Muzyki* (Music Lessons), 1969; *Fever and Other New Poems,* with an Introduction by Yevgeny Yevtushenko, translated by G. Dutton and I. Mezhakoff-Koriakin, 1969.

Anna Akhmatova (Anna Gorenko) b. Odessa, Russia, 1889; d. 1966. Her first books established her as a great Russian poet; remained in Stalinist Russia despite public humilitation and the imprisonment of her son; was expelled from the Writers' Union but was later readmitted and became its president. *Vecher* (Evening), 1912; *Anna Akhmatova: Selected Poems,* translated by Richard McKane, 1969; *Poems of Akhmatova,* selected and translated by Stanley Kunitz and Max Hayward, 1973; *A Poem Without a Hero,* translated by Carl R. Proffer with Assya Humesky, 1973.

Sophia de Mello Breyner Adresen b. Oporto, Portugal, 1919. Educated at Lisbon University; has published stories and translations as well as poetry. *Poesia* (Poetry), 1944, 2nd ed., 1959; *O Cristo cigano* (O Vagabond Christ), 1961; *Antologia 1944–1967* (Selected Works), 1968.

Katerina Anghelaki-Rooke b. Athens, Greece, 1939; studied literature at the University of Geneva. Spent a year in the U.S. with the International Writing Program at the University of Iowa in 1972. Has published translations of Dylan Thomas and Samuel Beckett. *Lykoi kai Synnepha* (Wolves and Clouds), 1963; *Poiemata* (Poems), 1971.

Odette Aslan b. Paris, France. Has been closely involved with the theater as actress, critic, and playwright; published study of Tagore; cofounder of the Club International de la Poésie (1957–1962). *Ascèse* (Ascesis), 1963; *Émergence* (Emergence), 1967.

Barbro Backberger b. Sweden, 1932. Has written both prose and poetry; member of a socialist feminist organization, and speaker for women's rights. *Goddag yxskaft* (Hello Axhandle), 1965.

Maria Banus b. Bucharest, Romania, 1914. Studied law and languages at the University of Bucharest. Journalist, poet, and playwright; has translated Goethe, Mayakovsky, Neruda, Hikmet, Rimbaud, and Browning. Has translated and edited an extensive anthology of love poetry. She has been published in the Seghers "Poetes d'aujourd'hui" series. *Tara fetelor* (The Land of Young Girls), 1937; *Se arată lumea* (The World Surges), 1956; *Tocmai ieşeam din arena* (Just As I Left the Arena), 1967; *Scrieri* (Works), 1971.

Ana Blandiana b. Timişoara, Romania, 1942. Studied philosophy at Cluj; editor and journalist in Bucharest. Published a collection of interviews, and in 1970 an "anti-journal," *Calitatea de martor* (Capacity for Witness). Has travelled extensively in Europe, and spent a year in the U.S. in 1973 at the University of Iowa in the International Writing Program. *Persoana întîa plural* (First Person Plural), 1964; *Octombrie, Noembrie, Decembrie* (October, November, December), 1972.

Karin Boye b. Sweden, 1900, d. 1941. Educated at the University of Uppsala. *För trädets skull* established her as one of the leading poets of her generation. She also wrote novels, one of which, *Kallocain*, was published in English (1966). In 1941, during the Second World War, she committed suicide. *Moln* (Clouds), 1922; *För trädets skull* (For the Sake of the Tree), 1935.

Julia de Burgos b. Carólina, Puerto Rico, 1914; d. New York, 1953. Grew up in a rural area of Puerto Rico; worked as a teacher and journalist. Her poetry, with its passionate identification with the oppressed, was virtually unrecognized in her lifetime. She suffered extreme poverty and died of alcoholism in New York. *Poema en veinte surcos* (Poem in Twenty Furrows), 1938; *Obra poetica* (Collected Works), 1961.

Nina Cassian b. Galați, Romania, 1924. Musician and composer as well as poet; studied at the University of Bucharest and the Conservatory of Music. Has translated works of Molière, Heine, Brecht; has won numerous prizes for her children's books. *La scara 1/1* (On the scale 1/1), 1947; *Versuri alese* (Selected Poems), 1955; *Disciplina harfei* (The Discipline of the Harp), 1964; *Loto Poeme* (Lottery Poems), 1972; *Anthology of Contemporary Romanian Poetry*, ed. MacGregor-Hastie (translations of some poems), 1969.

Cheng Min b. China, 1924? Studied philosophy at National Southwest University in Kunming during World War II, and English literature at Brown University in the early 1950's. Returned to People's Republic of China in 1959. *Shih chi* (Poems), 1949.

Marguerite Clerbout b. France. *De feuille en feuille au vent qui passe* (From Leaf to Leaf as the Wind Passes), 1938; *L'iris et l'oiseau* (The Iris and the Bird).

Lucha Corpi b. Veracruz, Mexico, 1945. Grew up in Saltillo, Mexico; now living in Oakland, California. Active in Chicano social movement; has worked with the Clínica de la Raza and in a program to teach English to Spanish-speaking women. *Fireflight* (with Elsie Alvarado de Ricord and Concha Michel), translated by Lucha Corpi and Catherine Rodriguez-Nieto, 1975.

Tove Ditlevsen b. Copenhagen, Denmark, 1918. Left school at fourteen to earn her living; her working-class background, three unsuccessful marriages, and drug addiction have been influences on her work. *Pige-*

sind (A Girl's Mind), 1939; *Kvindesind* (A Woman's Mind), 1955; *Det runde vaerelse* (The Round Room), 1973; *Collected Poems*, 1964.

Blaga Dmitrova b. Tirnovo, Bulgaria, 1922. Studied Slavic philology in Sofia. Attended Maxim Gorky Institute in Moscow. Editor of Poetry in Translation Department in Narodna Cultura Publishing House. Translator as well as poet, she has written two novels and several film scripts. *Journey to Oneself* appeared in English in 1969. *Svetut v shepa* (A World in Your Hand), 1962; *Ekspeditsiia kum idniia den* (Expedition into the Future), 1964.

Celia Dropkin b. Bobolsk, Russia, 1888; d. New York, 1956. Taught in Warsaw; emigrated to U.S. in 1912; wrote her early stories in Russian, but wrote in Yiddish from 1918. She was also a sculptor. *In Haysn Vint, Lider* (In the Hot Wind, Poems); *A Treasury of Yiddish Poetry*, ed. (Howe and Greenberg (translations of some poems), 1969.

Alda do Espírito Santo b. São Tomé, 1926. Was educated and has worked as a teacher in São Tomé e Príncipe, the former Portuguese colony off the coast of West Africa. Active in African nationalist groups, she was arrested and later imprisoned for political activity against the Portuguese colonial regime. *Modern Poetry from Africa*, ed. Moore and Beier (translations of some poems), 1968.

Forūgh Farrokhzād b. Teheran, Iran, 1935; died 1967. Published her first book of poetry at the age of eighteen; film-maker as well as poet; subjected to public criticism for her unorthodox life and work; travelled extensively in Europe; killed in an automobile accidnet. *Asir* (Prisoner), 1952; *Tavallodi Digar* (Another Birth), 1964; *Imān biyā-varim be-āgāze false sard* (Let Us Believe in the Coming of the Cold), 1974.

Gloria Fuertes b. Madrid, Spain, 1920. Has worked in radio, children's theater and as editor of children's magazines. Taught Spanish literature in the United States for three years. Her poetry is concerned with the struggle of the working classes and peasantry in Spain, and with the oppression of women. *Isla Ignorada* (Unknown Island), 1950; *Aconsejo Beber Hilo* (I Advise You to Drink Thread), 1954; *Antologia Poetica* (Selected Poetry), 1970.

Leah Goldberg b. Lithuania, 1911; d. Israel, 1970. Educated in a Hebrew school at Kovno and at the University of Bonn; emigrated to Palestine in 1935; appointed professor of comparative literature at Hebrew University, Jerusalem. Noted for extensive translations of European literature into Hebrew, and for her popular children's books; she has also written a novel and a play. *Tab'ot 'Ashan* (Rings of Smoke), 1935; *Barak Ba-Boker* (Lightning in the Morning), 1955; *Im Ha-Layla Ha-Zeh* (With This Night), 1964.

Natalya Gorbanevskaya b. U.S.S.R., 1936. Educated at Leningrad University. She has published mainly privately or abroad, with a few poems published by the authorized Soviet press. She took part in a demonstration against the invasion of Czechoslovakia and wrote an account of the trial that followed; she was then arrested and confined to a psychiatric prison ward in 1970. *Poems* (1969); *Poberezhe* (Seacoast), 1973; *Natalya Gorebanevskaya: Poems, The Trial, Prison,* edited and translated by Daniel Weissbort (1972).

Anne Hébert b. Sainte Catherine, Quebec, 1916. The publication of *Le tombeau des rois* established her reputation as a French-Canadian poet of major importance; she is also a novelist and short story writer, and has worked in television, theater, and film. Her novel *Kamouraska* has recently been made into a film. *Le tombeau des rois* (The Tomb of the Kings), 1953; also published in French and English with translation by Peter Miller, 1967; *Les songes en équilibre* (Dreams in Equilibrium), 1964.

Malka Heifetz Tussman b. Khaitscha, Ukraine, 1896. Emigrated to the United States in 1912. After her early poems in Russian and English, she decided to write in Yiddish, her native language. She has made translations into Yiddish of Akhmatova, Dylan Thomas, and Tagore. *Lider* (Poems), 1949; *Bletter Faln Nit* (Leaves Don't Fall), 1972.

Hien Luong b. Vietnam, mid-twentieth century. She was among a group of women taken as political prisoners to the notorious Con Son Prison Island in 1969. "Songs That Cannot Be Silenced" was composed in response to beatings the women suffered for singing liberation songs.

Maria Teresa Horta b. Lisbon, Portugal, 1937. Worked as literary editor for a major Lisbon newspaper. A novelist as well as poet, her novel *Hands on the Body* (1970) shocked official morality; the next year a book of her poems was banned. She stood trial in 1973 with Maria Velho da Costa and Maria Isabel Barreño on obscenity charges for publication of *New Portuguese Letters,* a collaborative work in mixed genres; following worldwide protest she was acquitted in 1974. She helped initiate the recent feminist movement in Portugal. *Jardim de Inverno* (Winter Garden), 1966; *Minha Senhora de Mim* (My Lady of Me), 1971.

Hsiung-hung ("Distant Rainbow," pen name of Hu Mei-tzu) b. 1940, Taiwan. She studied fine arts at the National Taiwan Normal University and now works as a designer in Taiwan. *Chin yung* (The Golden Chrysalis), 1968.

Majken Johansson b. Malmö, Sweden, 1930. Educated at the University of Lund. She has worked as a translator and critic, has been employed in a publishing house, and is a member of the Salvation Army. *Busk-teater* (Street Theater), 1952; *Collected Poems*, 1970.

Ingrid Jonker b. South Africa, 1933; d. 1965. One of the most important modern poets in Afrikaans. Her sympathy with the poor and oppressed led to difficulties with official censorship; her work was later widely recognized. Married and divorced, with one daughter; death by suicide. *Ontvlugting* (Escape), 1953; *Selected Poems*, translated by Jack Cope and William Plomer, 1968.

Amy Károlyi b. Budapest, Hungary, 1909. Studied languages at the University of Budapest. Published first work in literary journals in the 1930's; after the interruption of the war resumed publication in the '50's. Noted for her translations from Elizabethan English and Old German poetry; she has also translated Emily Dickinson and Sylvia Plath. *A harmadik ház* (The Third House), 1965; *Anti-mennyország* (Anti-Heaven), 1969; *-talen -telen* (in- un-), 1972.

Marie Luise Kaschnitz b. Karlsruhe, Germany, 1901. Known also as essayist and writer of short stories and radio plays, she is a professor of poetics at the University of Frankfurt. *Gedichte* (Poems), 1947; *Neue Gedichte* (New Poems), 1957; *Collected Poems*, 1965.

Caroline Ntseliseng 'Masechele Khaketla b. Lesotho, 1918. The first woman writer of Lesotho; played an important role in the movement to create a written literature in the tribal languages. Educated in Lesotho, she has worked as a teacher and is married to the writer and statesman B. M. Khaketla. *'Mantsopa*, 1963.

Venus Khoury b. Babda, Lebanon, 1937. Educated in Arab schools; studied political science at the Université Saint Joseph, Beirut. Has published a novel, *The Maladjusted*, 1972. Since 1972 has lived in Paris. *Visages inachevés* (Unfinished Faces), 1965; *Terres stagnantes* (Stagnant Lands), 1967; *Au sud du silence* (South of Silence), 1975.

Sarah Kirsch b. in Germany, 1935. Studied biology and worked in an agricultural cooperative. Later studied at the Literaturinstitut Johannes R. Becher; has translated Russian poets. Lives in East Germany. *Gespräch mit dem Saurier* (Conversation with the Saurian) with Rainer Kirsch, 1965; *Gedichte* (Poems), 1969.

Else Lasker-Schüler b. Elberfeld, Germany, 1869; d. Jerusalem, 1945. Of a middle-class Jewish family who encouraged her writing. Travelled through Europe with the poet Peter Hille. Read poems before the Alliance for Art, founded by her husband Georg Levin. Played a central role in German Expressionism. After her books were banned by the Nazis she fled to Switzerland and later to Jerusalem. *Styx* (Styx), 1902; *Collected Works* (10 vols.), 1920; Biography: *Else Lasker-Schüler, The Broken World,* by Hans W. Cohn, 1974.

Li Chü b. People's Republic of China, mid-twentieth century. She is a member of the farm commune of Ta Yeh District, Teng-fung county, Honan Province.

Nazik al-Malā'ikah b. Iraq, 1923. Studied Arabic and English literature at Baghdad University and Princeton; as poet and critic she has played a leading role in the Arab free verse movement; she has taught literature at major universities in the Middle East. *'Ashiqat al-layl* (In Love with the Night), 1947; *Diwān* (Collected Works), 1970–71; *An Anthology of Modern Arabic Poetry*, ed. Khouri and Algar (translations of some poems), 1974.

Eeva-Liisa Manner b. Finland, 1921. A major Finnish poet; her work was important in the consolidation of modernism in Finnish poetry in the 1950's. She has also written a novel, *Victors Beware*, about contemporary Spain, and a verse drama, *Eros and Psyche. Mustaa ja punaista* (Black and Red), 1944; *Orfiset laulut* (Orphic Songs), 1966; *Tämä matka* (This Journey), 1956; *Fahrenheit 121* (Fahrenheit 121), 1968; *Paetkaa purret kevein purjein* (Flee, Ships, with Light Sails), 1972.

Anna Margolin (Rosa Lebensbaum) b. Brest-Litovsk, Russia, 1887; d. New York, 1952. Married to Hebrew novelist Moses Stavsky; lived in United States and Israel. *Lider* (Poems), 1923; *A Treasury of Yiddish Poetry*, ed. Howe and Greenberg (translations of some poems), 1969.

Cecília Meireles b. Rio de Janeiro, Brazil, 1901; d. Rio de Janeiro 1964. A major Brazilian poet; twice nominated for the Nobel Prize; also a dramatist and translator of European and Indian writers into Portuguese. Has worked as a primary teacher, librarian, journalist, and professor of comparative literature; is a specialist in Brazilian folklore. *Espectros* (Spectres), 1919; *Obra Poetica* (Collected Works), 1958; *An Anthology of 20th Century Brazilian Poetry*, ed. Elizabeth Bishop and Emanuel Brasil (translations of some poems), 1972.

Máire Mhac an tSaoi b. Ireland, 1922. Well known as an Irish scholar and for her work in the cause of preservation of the Irish language. *Mairge na Saoire* (The Hiring Fair), 1956; *Codladh an Ghaisoigh* (Sleep of the Hero), 1973.

Gabriela Mistral (Lucila Godoy y Alcayaga) b. Vicuna, Chile, 1889; d. New York, 1957. Taught in rural schools in Chile and became a leader in innovative public education throughout Latin America. She was the first South American writer to receive the Nobel Prize for Literature, (1945). Represented Chile as consul in Spain, Portugal, France, Brazil, United States. Settled in U.S. in 1953. *Sonetos de la Muerte* (Sonnets of Death), 1914?, 1952; *Desolacion* (Despair), 1922; *Poesias completas* (Complete Works) ed. Margaret Bates, 1966; *Selected Poems of Gabriela Mistral*, translated and edited by Langston Hughes, 1957;

Selected Poems of Gabriela Mistral, translated and edited by Doris Dana, 1971; Biography: *Gabriela Mistral,* by Carmen Conde, 1970.

Kadia Molodowsky b. Lithuania, 1893. Taught in Warsaw where her socialist writings incurred attack by the Fascists and forced her emigration (1935) to New York. Made long visits to Israel; her work shows both American and Israeli influences. Noted also as novelist and writer of children's poetry, and editor of *Sevive,* an important Yiddish literary magazine. *Heshvendike Nekht* (Nights of Heshven), 1927; *Kinder Maaselakh* (Children's Stories), 1930; *Likht Fun Dornboym* (Light from the Thornbush), 1965; *Onions and Cucumbers and Plums,* ed. F. Z. Betsky (translations of some poems), 1958.

Mririda n'Ait Attik b. Magdaz, Morocco, fl. 1940–45; d. ? Born in a Berber village in the Tassaout valley of the Atlas Mountains. She was famous during World War II a a courtesan-poet-singer in the *souk* of Azilal, Morocco. Her songs, composed in the Berber dialect of *tachelhait* and based on oral traditions, were collected and translated into French by René Euloge, a French soldier. After the war she disappeared from Azilal. *The Songs of Mririda,* translated by Daniel Halpern and Paula Paley, 1974.

Ada Negri b. Lodi, Italy, 1870; d. Milan, Italy, 1945. Her work is marked by the economic misery of an impoverished childhood, later by an unhappy love affair and an unsuccessful marriage. A schoolteacher, later a college professor, she lived in Switzerland for some years, returning to Italy in 1914. Nominated to Italian Academy, 1940. *Fatalità* (*Fate,* translated by A. M. von Blomberg, 1898), 1892; *Fons Amoris 1939–43* (Fount of Love 1939–43), 1946.

Ágnes Nemes Nagy b. Budapest, Hungary, 1922. Studied Hungarian and Latin literature at the University of Budapest, and taught from 1953–1957. She belonged to the group of anti-romantic poets who were called "lyrical objectivists." Known as an outstanding translator of French classical drama. *Kettős világban* (In the Second World), 1946; *Szárazvillám* (Heat Lightning), 1957; *A lovak és az angyalok* (Horses and Angels), 1969.

Nuala ní Dhomhnaill b. Lanchashire, England, 1952. Sent to Kerry Gaeltacht (Irish-speaking area) to learn Irish. Her work has appeared in Irish periodicals.

Violeta Parra b. San Carlos, Chile, 1917; d. Chile, 1967. She was a poet–folk-singer of great originality, and is famous throughout Latin America; besides composing and recording her own songs, she collected and recorded many of the traditional folk songs of Chile; also an accomplished potter and weaver; death by suicide. *La Poésie Populaire des Andes* (Popular Poetry of the Andes), 1964; *Decimas* (Stanzas), 1970; records.

Ping-hsin ("Ice-Heart," pen name of Hsieh Wan-ying) b. Fukien, China, 1902. Educated at missionary schools in Peking, and at Yenching University and Wellesley; she later taught at Yenching. After living in Japan, in 1951 she returned to the People's Republic where she was active in the Communist literary movement before the Cultural Revolution in 1964. Member of Japanese Delegation from the People's Republic in 1971. She has published numerous novels, essays, and works for children, but little poetry since the twenties. *Fan hsing* (Multitudinous Stars), 1921, *Ch'un shui* (Spring Waters), 1922; *Ping-hsin shih chi* (The Poetry of Ping-hsin), 1932; *Twentieth Century Chinese Poetry: an Anthology*, ed. Kai-yu Hsu (translations of some poems), 1963.

Veronica Porumbacu b. Bucharest, Romania, 1921. Educated at the University of Bucharest; professor of comparative literature. She has translated extensively from Hungarian, English, and French, and has translated and edited an anthology of Scandanavian poetry, plus an international anthology of poetry by women. An autobiographical novel *Portile* (Gateways) was published in 1968. *Visele Babei Dochia* (Dreams of Old Dokia), 1947; *Poezii, selectie retrospectivă* (Poetry, a Retrospective Selection), 1962; *Cere* (Ask), 1971.

Antonia Pozzi b. Milan, Italy, 1912; d. Italy, 1938. Educated at the University of Milan. After her deat by suicide her family published her journal of poetry, composed between her seventeenth and twenty-sixth year; her poems have been translated into German, French and Romanian. *Parole* (Words), 1939.

Amrita Pritam b. India, 1919. In addition to poetry she has published fourteen novels, six collections of short stories, several collections of folk songs, plus essays, travelogues, and an autobiography; a major writer in the Punjabi language. Editor and publisher of *naagmanii* (The Jewelled Serpent) a journal of Punjabi liteature. Lives presently in New Delhi. *ThaNDiyaaN kirnaaN* (Cool Rays), 1935; *naagmanii* (The Jewelled Serpent), 1964; *Selected Poems,* ed. Pritish Nandy and translated by Khushwant Singh and others, 1970; *Existence and Other Poems,* translated by Mahendra Kulasreshta, 1968; *Black Rose,* translated by Charles Brasch with Amrita Pritam, 1967.

Dahlia Ravikovitch b. Tel Aviv, Israel, 1936. Raised on a collective farm; educated in Haifa; served a short time in the army; studied English literature at the Hebrew University in Jerusalem. Ahavat Tapuakh Ha-Zahav (The Love of an Orange), 1959; *Kol Mishbareha Vo-Galekha* (All Thy Breakers and Waves), 1972; *A Dress of Fire,* selected poems translated by Chana Bloch, 1976.

Anna Rydstedt-Dannstedt b. Öland, Sweden, 1928. Educated at University of Lund. Teaches at Folkhögskolan (Free/Popular University) in Stockholm. *Lökvår* (Onion Spring), 1957; *Presensbarn* (Child of the Present), 1964.

Nelly Sachs b. Berlin, Germany, 1891; d. Stockholm, Sweden, 1970. Of an assimilated Jewish family; studied dance and music. She lived in seclusion and fear during the Nazi regime preceding her escape to Stockholm in 1940. Besides poetry, she has composed a series of plays she called "Scenic Poetry." She received the Nobel Prize for Literature in 1966. *In den Wohnungen des Todes* (In the Habitations of Death), 1947; *Nelly Sachs/O The Chimneys*, selected poems, including *Eli*, a verse play; translated from the German by Michael Hamburger, Christopher Holme, Ruth and Matthew Mead, Michael Roloff, 1967; *The Seeker, and Other Poems* (in English), 1970.

Saniya Sālih b. Damascus, Syria, 1939. Has published widely in literary journals in Lebanon and Syria. Lives in Damascus with her husband, Muhammad al-Maghout, also a poet. *Al-zamān al-dayyiq* (Pressed Time), 1964; *Hibr al I'dām* (The Ink of Execution), 1970.

Ann Smith b. Bohuslän, Sweden, 1930. Member of the Writer's Union. Has achieved recognition and popularity in Sweden. *Två i stjärnan* (Two in the Star), 1963; *Sinnlighetens tecken* (The Emblem of Sensuality), 1972.

Edith Södergran b. St. Petersburg, Russia. d. in Finland, 1923. Of Swedish-speaking Finnish parents, she was educated at a German high school and lived in a mixed Finnish Russian district in St. Petersburg, returning to Finland after the Russian Revolution. She wrote in Swedish and is considered a major modern poet in Finland and in Sweden. Ill with tuberculosis from age eighteen, she spent much time in sanatoria before her death. *Dikter* (Poems), 1916; *Septemberlyran* (The Lyre of September), 1918; *Landet som icke är* (The Land That Is Not) edited posthumously by Elmer Diktonius, 1925; *Collected Poems,* edited by G. Tideström, 1949; *Seven Swedish Poets* (translations of some poems), 1963.

Noémia da Sousa (also pseudonym *Vera Micaia*) b. Lourenço Marques, Mozambique, 1927. Attended secondary school in Brazil; lived for some years in Lisbon until in 1964 she was forced to seek refuge in France because of her activities against the Salazar regime in Portugal. Her work has appeared in periodicals in Angola, Mozambique, Brazil, France, and in many anthologies of African poetry. *Modern Poetry from Africa,* ed. Moore and Beier (translations of some poems), 1968.

Alfonsina Storni b. Switzerland, 1892; d. Argentina, 1938. Grew up in the provinces of San Juan and Santa Fé, Argentina. Earned her own living from the age of thirteen in theater, later as teacher, business-woman, journalist, playwright. Incurably ill, she drowned herself in the Mar del Plata. *La inquietud del rosal* (Restless Rosebush), 1916; *Antologia poetica* (Selected Poems), 1940; *Obra poetica* (Poetry), 1948.

Margit Szécsi b. Budapest, Hungary, 1928. Of a working class back-ground; she studied two years at Budapest University; has worked briefly as a bricklayer, editor, and as director of a provincial cultural center; since 1953 she has worked as freelance writer. *Marcius* (March), 1955; *Új Heraldika* (New Herald), 1967; *Szent Buborék* (Saint Bubbles), 1974.

Teresa Torres. No information available.

Marina Tsvetayeva b. Russia, 1892; d. Yelabuga, Russia, 1941. Educated in Russia, Germany and France. After her marriage she lived abroad in Prague, Berlin and Paris. She returned to Russia in 1939 where her husband was alleged to be a spy and shot. Evacuted to Yelabuga, her son killed in action, her daughter arrested, and unable to find work, she hanged herself. *Vechernii al'bom* (Evening Album), 1910; *Posle Rosii* (After Russia) 1922–25 (1928); *Izbrannoye* (Selection), 1961; *Izbranniye proizbedeniya* (Selected Works), 1965; Biography: *Marina Cvetaeva: Her Life and Art* by Simon Karlinsky, 1966.

Nadia Tuéni b. Beirut, Lebanon, 1935. Educated in French schools in Greece and Lebanon; law degree from Université Saint Joseph in Beirut; journalist for *An-Nahar*. Composed story and scenario for *Faramane*, a drama produced for the International Festival of Baalbeck (1970). In 1973 she received the Prix de l'Académie Francaise. *Les Textes Blonds* (Blond Texts), 1963; *Le Reveur de Terre* (Dreamer of the Earth), 1975.

Fadwa Tuqān b. Nablus, Palestine, 1917. A leader in the modernist movement in Arab poetry and an innovator in form and subject matter. Since 1967, her poetry has become increasingly political in theme. *Wajadtuha* (I Found It), 1962; *Al-Fida'i wa al-ard* (The Guerrilla and the Land), 1968; *An Anthology of Modern Arabic Poetry*, ed. Khouri and Algar (translations of some poems), 1974.

Isabelle Vuckovic b. France. Born in a small town in the province of Landes and educated at the University of Bordeaux. She lived in Spain for several years where her first collection of poetry was published; also a novelist. *Amour, Svelte Rodeur* . . . (Love, Svelte Prowler . . .), 1957.

Ellen Warmond b. Holland, 1930. Associated with a group of experi-mental poets in Holland called "The '50'ers." Works for the Dutch Lit-erary Museum in the Hague. Her work has appeared in translation in two anthologies of Dutch and Flemish poets published by Twowindows Press in Berkeley: *Change of Scene* (1969) and *The Shape of Houses: Women's Voices from Holland and Flanders* (1974).

Simone Weil b. Paris, 1909; d. Kent, England, 1943. Of Jewish parentage, she became a brilliant professor of philosophy and mathematics, and a devout but unorthodox Christian. Her commitment to the oppressed led her to do farm and factory labor. Fought in Spanish Civil War. Emigrated to U.S. in 1942 with her parents, but returned to England to help the Free French. Died of fatigue and malnutrition. An original thinker and essayist. *La pesanteur et la grace* (*Gravity and Grace*); *L'attente de dieu* (*Waiting for God*), 1949; *L'enracinement* (*The Need for Roots*), 1949–50; *Cahiers* (*Notebooks*), 1951–56 (all four appear in English under these titles); "The Iliad, or the Poem of Force," translated by Mary McCarthy; Biography: *La Vie de Simone Weil*, by Simone Petrement, 2 vols., 1973.

Yosano Akiko b. Sakai, Japan, 1878; d. Japan 1942. Of middle-class background, she was largely self-educated. Her earliest work created scandal because of its sexual explicitness, but her themes became popular with other young poets and the period 1904–9 was called the "Age of Akiko." She advocated education for women and founded a girls' school. *Midaregami* (Tangled Hair), 1901; *Yosano Akiko Zenshu* (Collected Works of Yosano Akiko) 14 vols., 1972; *Three Women Poets of Modern Japan,* translations by Glenn Hughes and Yozan T. Iwasaki, 1927; *Tangled Hair,* translated by Shio Sakanishi, 1935, also translated by Sanford Goldstein and Seishi Shinoda, 1970; *The Poetry of Yosano Akiko,* translations by H. H. Honda, 1957.

The Editors

Joanna Bankier
Born in Warszaw, Poland, in 1939; educated in Sweden and France. M.A. in Comparative Literature, Sorbonne, Paris. Completing a Ph.D. in Comparative Literature, University of California, Berkeley. Has taught Swedish language and literature in the Scandinavian Department at the University of California, Berkeley. Has translated poetry from Polish, Swedish, and French. Co-editor of an international, historical anthology of women poets.

Carol Cosman
Born in Boston in 1943. She has an M.A. in English from the University of California, Berkeley, where she has taught courses on women and fiction with the Extension Curriculum. She has translated *The Old and the New from Don Quixote to Kafka*, by Marthe Robert (Berkeley, 1976), and is currently working on a biography of Stendhal with her husband, Robert Alter.

Doris Earnshaw
Born in Toronto, Canada. She is currently completing a Ph.D. in medieval studies in the Department of Comparative Literature, University of California, Berkeley, and teaching in the Department of Rhetoric. She is founder of the Berkeley Dante Society and co-editor of a historical anthology of women poets.

Joan Keefe
Born in Kildare, Ireland. Graduate of the University of Ireland and the University of California, Berkeley. Her poetry and translations from the Irish have appeared in many Irish, British, and American periodicals, as well as in *The Anthology of New Irish Poetry* (1972–74) and the *Pan Anthology of Modern Irish Poetry* (1975). She is the editor and translator of *Irish Poems, from Cromwell to the Famine: A Miscellany* (1976).

213

Deirdre Lashgari

Born Ann Arbor, Michigan, in 1941. M.A. in English and Near Eastern Languages. Completing a dissertation in Comparative Literature on British women novelists. Taught literature and women's studies at the University of California and the University of Teheran. Preparing a collection of her translations of modern Persian poetry and fiction. Currently working with the Berkeley Free Clinic and co-editing a forthcoming international, historical anthology of women poets.

Kathleen Weaver

Born 1945. M.A. in Comparative Literature, University of California, Berkeley; also studied in Paris and Edinburgh. Has taught courses on poetry and women's literature as well as on women and film. Also editor of *The Film Programmer's Guide to 16mm Rentals*, 2nd edition; co-editor of a historical survey of women poets and an anthology of poetry about the coup in Chile, *Chile Sí.*

Index